AF540824

FOOD SERVICE

LAYOUT, DESIGN AND THEORY

FOOD SERVICE
LAYOUT, DESIGN AND THEORY

By

William Lever

DISCOVERY PUBLISHING HOUSE PVT. LTD.
NEW DELHI-110 002

Published by:
Tilak Wasan

DISCOVERY PUBLISHING HOUSE PVT. LTD.
4831/24, Prahlad Street, Ansari Road
Darya Ganj, New Delhi-110002 (India)
Phone : +91-11-23279245, 43764432
Fax : +91-11-23253475
E-mail : parul.wasan@gmail.com
discoverypublishinghouse@gmail.com
info@discoverypublishinggroup.com
web : www.discoverypublishinggroup.com

***First Edition:* 2011**
ISBN: 978-81-8356-932-3

Food Service: ***Layout, Design and Theory***

Printed at:
Mehra Offset Press
Delhi

PREFACE

The food service industry is one of the largest employers in the United States. Over 805,360 people are currently working as servers and managers alone. 59% of these workers are under the age of 30, and over 66% hold only a high school diploma or less. A food service designer has expertise in the design and layout of your commercial kitchen and dining room complete with equipment specified for your specific concept, and will consult with you in ways to save you money when it comes to what equipment you need, where to place the electrical and plumbing, and will provide for you all the necessary drawings, plans and specifications needed for the city, the contractors and equipment companies.

An early, inexpensive form of bottle service ($90, compared with $6 drinks) was established at the *Tunnel* in 1993 (by Jeffrey Jah and Mark Baker). The modern form of bottle service was pioneered in 1995 by Michael Ault at *Spy Bar* and in 1996, *Chaos* ($175 for a bottle of Stolichnaya vodka), with the express goal of creating a "barrier to entry", rather than of increasing liquor sales. The concept later spread to other American cities, notably Miami and Las Vegas in the early 2000s.

The foodservice industry includes restaurants, school and hospital cafeterias, catering operations, and many other formats. The companies that supply foodservice operators are called foodservice distributors. The foodservice industry is one of the largest employers in the United States. Over 805,360 people are currently working as servers and managers alone. 59% of these workers are under the age of 30, and over 66% hold only a high school diploma or less. Foodservice distributors sell goods like small wares (kitchen utensils) and bulk foods. Some companies manufacture products in both consumer and foodservice versions. The consumer version usually comes in individual-sized packages with elaborate label design for retail sale. The foodservice version is packaged in a much larger industrial size and often lacks the colorful label designs of the consumer version.

—Author

Contents

Chapter–1

Design and Layout of Food Service Facilities

Food service managers oversee the day-to-day running of restaurants, bars and "other establishments that prepare and serve meals and beverages to customers" according to the U.S. Department of Labor (DOL). Food service managers handle "all of the administrative and human-resource functions of running the business, including recruiting new employees and monitoring employee performance and training." They also work to make sure that customers are happy with their dining experience.

So you have an idea for a restaurant... or maybe this is even your second or third. Each time you wonder, now who do I contact first? What's the difference between architectural services and those of a food service designer?

It's good that you are asking, because you may or may not even need an architect on the job. If you are looking to stay within a budget, (and who isn't?), then even though some of their services overlap, architect fees are higher than a food service designer right out of the shoot. However, that said, in most cases you need at the least an architect stamp on your plans, and at the most you need an architect to design the structure of the building or your part of the building.

So, what does that mean?

A food service designer has expertise in the design and layout of your commercial kitchen and dining room complete with equipment specified for your specific concept, and will consult with you in ways to save you money when it comes to what equipment you need, where to place the electrical and plumbing, and will provide for you all the necessary drawings, plans and specifications needed for the city, the contractors and equipment companies.

On the otherhand, the architect can do all this for you, but you want to be sure to hire one that has experience in restaurant operations, restaurant equipment, flow and layout of restaurants. There are many architects with this specialty. So what's the difference in that case? The fee. Bottom line is the fee.

The architect has expertise in designing structure, which the food service designer does not. If that is not an issue, for instance if you are going into a space that has already been built or is already designed by an architect then you will save money going to an independent food service designer and consultant for the food service layout of the space designed by the architect.

When designing and laying out a restaurant, bar or other food-service space, these are among the most important questions faced -even the experienced restaurateur may be without definite answers.

For the designer or office manager laying out a break room, these questions can be even more mystifying. The answer selected can (literally) make or break operational success. Night after night, having on two top restaurant tables available with parties of six or eight waiting or having your banquets that seat six regularly filled with lone couples enjoying romantic dinners can drive you broke!

There is no panacea for all of these issues - We do not have a single magic formula (or even a magic eight ball) to answer the questions, but we have gathered some useful information and research results to assist you in working out the best answer for you.

The *Frequently Asked Questions* below may answer some questions about the mix and spacing of restaurant tables but may actually raise more questions - if so, it has accomplishes its purpose as it can lead to the optimal restaurant table mix, table spacing. restaurnt design and best layout for YOU.

Diner, server and busser traffic patterns should be considered when designing restaurant table layout. That number of passes (volume), speed of travel (rate), distance traveled to and around restaurant tables, and direction of flow should be mapped and considered in restaurant design.

If fast service is more critical to your restaurant success, pay attention to distance from the back to the front of the re-starant dining room layout and vice versa. Quick service restaurant and cafeteria design should have at least a partial focus on access and speed of accessibility. These fast-paced operations should have clear paths for travel with optimal economy and as little crossing as possible. Don't become frustrated or upset, just consider this in your restaurant floor plan layout.

In slower paced environments, hostess stations should be close enough to the front door so that they are easily visible and obvious but not so close as to cause congestion at ingress and egress points of the restaurant. If large parties are promoted and desired, the size of and flow through the restaurant waiting area can become crucial. If people waiting are steered towards the bar by design, remember that the noise level, congestion and sometimes smoke level will be higher here and in the areas of your restaurant floor plan surrounding the bar. an in the general dining area.

The waiting area should be comfortable but not too much so as you don't typically want people to sink in as resist or resent being seated at their restaurant tables.

For a cafe, the top considerations are different - you don't want people too comfortable or private as you want them to move on after a meal. A floorplan with a cafe table layout creating slight crowding might be the winner.

In design of a restaurant waiting area or a cafe floor plan (cafe design), you want your busboys to be able to get in and out, quickly clearing and cleaning for new patrons.

FOOD COURT FURNITURE AND DÉCOR

A Palmer Hamilton Food Court transforms your cafeteria into a relaxed environment, providing a unique and comfortable place to dine and interact. Palmer Hamilton offers a wide selection of furniture and custom décor to complement your current cafeteria.

Palmer Hamilton walks you through the entire process, from design to furniture selection to customized artwork, crowd-control systems, installation services and more. You have full access to our talented design team with over 100 years of combined experience in food service facilities design.

Transform your cafeteria into an exciting and vibrant dining environment.

FOOD COURT BENEFITS

Food Courts offer convenient, casual campus dining giving students a variety of both traditional and non-traditional cafeteria elements. From booths to high-top chairs, to lounge furniture and décor, Food Courts provide a unique and comfortable place to dine and interact. They are a proven way to keep students on campus and involved in your food service program, which means increased revenue for your school. Other benefits include:

- Increase student participation.
- Increase revenue and profits.
- Transform your cafeteria into an exciting and enticing environment for diversified students to all enjoy.
- Enhance school pride and foster a sense of community between students.
- Accommodate more students with increased seating.
- Reduce student congestion with improved traffic flow.
- Provide a community center/gathering place for all students, faculty and parents.
- Introduce catering opportunities for outside groups.

Payback Analysis

Research has shown that food courts will pay off by recapturing initial investments in about 18 months for a 2,000 student middle or high school, with profits continuing after the initial payback period. Schools that have made this transformation have experienced profit increases up to 74%, with the majority of schools averaging over a 25% increase.

The following example chart shows possible increases in revenue based on the various percentages of increase. The below K-12 model is based on 1,300 total students enrolled and currently serving 500 students *(Note: Analysis is based on a 180 day school year and average student spending of $2.88 per day).*

Increased Student Participation	15%	25%	35%	45%
Number of Student Increase	195	325	455	585
Annual Revenue Increases	$101,088	$168,480	$235,872	$303,264

A Palmer Hamilton Food Court is the perfect on-campus dining solution for any food service program.

A Well-designed Cafeteria

With an emphasis on interactive design, variety and comfort, food courts can create a multitude of environments by incorporating free-standing tables, booth seating, custom cabinets and a full range of décor and accessories. Components of a Well-designed Cafeteria take into consideration:

Age & Cultural Appropriateness—Each design will reflect the age and culture of the students, aligning with the identity of the school.

Furniture Selection—Ranging from lounge furniture to mobile tables, booths to high-top tables, the chosen furniture helps reflect the atmosphere of the food court.

Paint Schemes—Brighten up a dull lunchroom with custom paint schemes to resemble a restaurant-style eating area rather than an institutional cafeteria.

Décor Themes—Décor such as graphics, lighting, and banner are great tools to use to entice students to stay on campus for lunch.

Furniture Layout—The right furniture layout brings additional seating, improves functionality and adds excitement and depth to any cafeteria.

Traffic Flow—Well designed food courts can increase student flow, reduce theft and minimize congestion in the cafeteria.

Our Design Process

Palmer Hamilton's professional design group will walk you through the entire food court process. You will have full access to the best design team in the industry, with over 100 years of combined expertise in food service facilities design. If you have a new building or an older campus that needs a cutting-edge Food Court, we can provide the design services that will be your Blueprint for Success.

Step 1 - Pre-design Consulation—We begin the process of creating a food court concept for your facility by understanding your basic needs and goals. Pre-design consultation includes school site inspection and analysis, student and staff interviews, budget reviews and timeline projections.

Step 2 - Design & Plan—With our staff of professional food court designers, we provide the artistic skill, creativity and knowledge to create the concept while maximizing the functionality of your school cafeteria. Design and plan includes seating layout, furniture selection, graphic design, color selection, custom cabinets and millwork, wall-mounted graphics, décor and signage designs.

Step 3 - Design Proposal—A member of our food court design team will present and describe the cafeteria design concept enabling you to visualize the final food court layout and design. The design proposal will include rendered floor plans, rendered elevations, décor illustrations, presentation boards, room finishes, and final specification documents.

Turn-key Project Management

Once you have approved your food court design a personal project manager will coordinate, develop and manage your project from start to finish, including all phases of your cafeteria transformation.

Turn-key Project Management Includes:

- Organizing final design documents
- Working with you to issue a purchase order
- Coordinating and tracking all production
- Arranging product delivery
- Coordinating installation teams
- Conducting final walk-through inspection

Plan for Construction

Design as a noun informally refers to a plan for the construction of an object or a system (as in architectural blueprints, engineering drawing, business process, circuit diagrams and sewing patterns) while "to design" (verb) refers to making this plan. No generally-accepted definition of "design" exists, and the term has different connotations in different fields. However, one can also design by directly constructing an object as in pottery, engineering, management, cowboy coding and graphic design.

Here, a "specification" can be manifested as either a plan or a finished product and "primitives" are the elements from which the design object is composed. With such a broad denotation, there is no universal language or unifying institution for designers of all disciplines. This allows for many differing philosophies and approaches toward the subject

The person designing is called a *designer*, which is also a term used for people who work professionally in one of the various design areas, usually also specifying which area is being dealt with (such as a *fashion designer*, *concept designer* or *web designer*). A designer's sequence of activities is called a design process. The scientific study of design is called design science.

Designing often necessitates considering the aesthetic, functional, economic and sociopolitical dimensions of both the design object and design process. It may involve considerable research, thought, modeling, interactive adjustment, and re-design. Meanwhile, diverse kinds of objects may be designed, including clothing, graphical user interfaces, skyscrapers, corporate identities, business processes and even methods of designing.

Design as a Process

Substantial disagreement exists concerning how designers in many fields, whether amateur or professional, alone or in teams, produce designs. Dorst and Dijkhuis argued that "there are many ways of describing design processes" and discussed "two basic and fundamentally different ways", both of which have several names. The prevailing view has been called "The Rational Model", "Technical Problem Solving" and "The Reason-Centric Perspective". The alternative view has been called "Reflection-in-Action" "co-evolution" and "The Action-Centric Perspective".

The Rational Model

The Rational Model was independently developed by Simon and Pahl and Beitz. It posits that:

1. designers attempt to optimize a design candidate for known constraints and objectives,
2. the design process is plan-driven,
3. the design process is understood in terms of a discrete sequence of stages.

The Rational Model is based on a rationalist philosophy and underlies the Waterfall Model, Systems Development Life Cycle and much of the engineering design literature.

Example Sequence of Stages

Typical stages consistent with The Rational Model include the following :

- Pre-production design
  - Design brief or Parti – an early (often the beginning) statement of design goals
  - Analysis – analysis of current design goals
  - Research – investigating similar design solutions in the field or related topics
  - Specification – specifying requirements of a design solution for a product (product design specification) or service.
  - Problem solving–conceptualizing and documenting design solutions
  - Presentation – presenting design solutions
- Design during production
  - Development – continuation and improvement of a designed solution
  - Testing – in situ testing a designed solution
- Post-production design feedback for future designs
  - Implementation–introducing the designed solution into the environment
  - Evaluation and conclusion – summary of process and results, including constructive criticism and suggestions for future improvements
- Redesign – any or all stages in the design process repeated (with corrections made) at any time before, during, or after production.

Each stage has many associated best practices.

CRITICISM OF THE RATIONAL MODEL

The Rational Model has been widely criticized on two primary grounds :

1. Designers do not work this way–extensive empirical evidence has demonstrated that designers do not act as the rational model suggests.

2. Unrealistic assumptions – goals are often unknown when a design project begins, and the requirements and constraints continue to change.

The Action-Centric Model

The Action-Centric Perspective is a label given to a collection of interrelated concepts, which are antithetical to The Rational Model. It posits that:

1. Designers use creativity and emotion to generate design candidates,
2. The design process is improvised,
3. No universal sequence of stages is apparent – analysis, design and implementation are contemporary and inextricably linked

The Action-Centric Perspective is a based on an empiricist philosophy and broadly consistent with the Agile approach and amethodical development. Substantial empirical evidence supports the veracity of this perspective in describing the actions of real designers.

Food Service

Food Service (US English) or catering industry (British English) defines those businesses, institutions, and companies responsible for any meal prepared outside the home. This industry includes restaurants, school and hospital cafeterias, catering operations, and many other formats.

The companies that supply food service operators are called food service distributors. Food Service distributors sell goods like small wares (kitchen utensils) and foods. Some companies manufacture products in both consumer and food service versions. The consumer version usually comes in individual-sized packages with elaborate label design for retail sale. The food service version is packaged in a much larger industrial size and often lacks the colorful label designs of the consumer version.

Providers

Food service sales to restaurants and institutions are estimated to be approximately $400 billion, about equal with consumer sales of foods through grocery outlets. Major food service providers include Aramark, Brinker International, Compass Group, the Crown Group, Darden Restaurants, Sysco, McLane Company, US Food service and 3663 First for Food service.

Employment Statistics

The food service industry is one of the largest employers in the United States. Over 805,360 people are currently working as servers and managers alone. 59% of these workers are under the age of 30, and over 66% hold only a high school diploma or less.

Counter Service

Counter service is a form of service in restaurants, pubs, and bars where food or drinks are ordered at the counter. Counter service is also called "bar service" in the case of pubs and bars where the counter is also called the bar. Counter service is compared with table service where service is provided at the table. With counter service, the customer generally pays before consuming the food or drink. Some fast food restaurants offer only counter service while table service is the common form in most restaurants. For pubs and bars, bar service is the norm in the United Kingdom and the Republic of Ireland whereas table service is the norm in the United States and Continental Europe.

Table Service

Table service is food service served to the customer's table by waiters and waitressess, also known as "servers".

Table service is the norm in most restaurants, while for some fast food restaurants counter service is the common form. For pubs and bars, table service is the norm in the United States whereas counter service is the norm in the United Kingdom. With table service, the customer generally pays at the end of meal. Various methods of table service can be provided. See, for instance, silver service.

Gueridon Service

Gueridon service is a form of food service provided by restaurants to their guests. This type of service encompasses preparing food (primarily salads, main dishes such as beef stroganoff, or desserts) in direct view of the guests, using a "Gueridon". A gueridon typically consists of a trolley that is well equipped to prepare, cook and serve the food to the guest. There will be a gas hob, chopping board, cutlery drawer, cold store (depending on the trolley type) and general working area.

Bottle Service

Bottle service is a feature of many upscale bars and nightclubs where patrons may purchase entire bottles of liquor for their personal consumption.The purchase of bottle service typically includes a reserved table for the patron's party and mixers of the patron's choice. Bottle service can include the service of a VIP host, who will ensure that patrons have sufficient mixers and will often make drinks using the patrons' liquor bottle and mixers. The purchase of bottle service sometimes results in cover charge being waived for the purchaser's party, and often allows patrons to bypass entrance lines.

The cost of a bottle at such a bar or club is usually extremely marked up, often by 2000% or more (20×), and can account for a significant portion of an establishment's revenue. Early forms of bottle service existed in World

War II era Japan, where unfinished bottles would be stored. In its modern form, an early example was in 1988 at the Paris nightclub *Les Bains Douches,* bottle service was introduced to deal with an excess of customer demand.

An early, inexpensive form of bottle service ($90, compared with $6 drinks) was established at the *Tunnel* in 1993 (by Jeffrey Jah and Mark Baker). The modern form of bottle service was pioneered in 1995 by Michael Ault at *Spy Bar* and in 1996, *Chaos* ($175 for a bottle of Stolichnaya vodka), with the express goal of creating a "barrier to entry", rather than of increasing liquor sales. The concept later spread to other American cities, notably Miami and Las Vegas in the early 2000s.

Waiting Staff

Waiting staff, wait staff, or waitstaff are those who work at a restaurant or a bar attending customers — supplying them with food and drink as requested. Traditionally, a male waiting tables is called a "waiter" and a female a "waitress" with the gender-neutral version being a "server". Other gender-neutral versions include using "*waiter*" indiscriminately for males and females, "*waitperson*", or the Americanism "*waitron*", which was coined in the 1980s.

Waiting on tables is (along with nursing and teaching) part of the service sector, and among the most common occupations in the United States. The Bureau of Labor Statistics estimates that, as of May 2008, there were over 2.2 million persons employed as servers in the U.S. Many servers are required by their employers to wear a uniform.

Duties of Waiting Staff

The duties of waiting staff include preparing tables for a meal, taking customers' orders, serving drinks and food, and cleaning up before, after and during servings in a restaurant. Silver service staff are specially trained to serve at banquets or high-end restaurants. They follow specific rules of service and it is a skilled job. They generally wear black and white with a long, white apron (extending from the waist to ankle).

The head server is in charge of the waiting staff, and is also frequently responsible for assigning seating. The functions of a head server can overlap to some degree with that of the maître d'hôtel. Some restaurants employ busboys or busgirls, increasingly referred to as bussers, to clear dirty dishes, set tables, and otherwise assist the waiting staff.

Tipping

In the United States, United Kingdom, Canada, many other Western countries and parts of the Middle East, it is customary for customers to pay a tip to a server after a meal, with a possible range from 15% to 30% depending on the level and quality of service. In some situations, a tip or "service charge" will be included on the restaurant bill in the U.S.

Also called a gratuity, a "service charge" will be automatically applied for situations where the restaurant management imposes this to ensure that the servers working in such situations earn their usual tip income. Such service charges are usually around 18%; an additional voluntary tip is sometimes given.

There is some debate in the U.S. whether a "minimum tip" exists as a convention; some argue that 15% or 20% is a minimum tip or that it is extremely rude to not leave at least $1, even if the service was not up to standard. However, some people also believe that a "minimum tip" is a way for employers to shift the responsibility of paying employee wages onto the customer. These issues are regional, cultural, and very subjective.

In Germany and other Western countries, where minimum wages exist for servers and where tipping is not culturally entrenched, most tips take the form of rounding up to the nearest whole or half denomination of currency when the server is cashing a party out at their table. In the United Kingdom it is common practice to tip 10% of the cost of the meal.

By contrast, servers in Japan refuse tips because it isn't a Japanese custom.

Tipping is not customary in Asia, Australia and New Zealand and is not factored into wages of staff, however tips may be appreciated. This is especially the case if the customer or party has been unusually difficult or has left a mess - parents of small children, for example, may leave a small tip. In these countries, tips are often placed into a Tip Jar and pooled rather than being kept by individual servers. This money is usually then spent on things that directly benefit staff - it may be used to maintain staff facilities or to fund events such as Christmas parties, for example.

In Taiwan and Hong Kong, a 10% service fee is often added to meals in middle-to-upscale restaurants. However, this fee does not go to the waitstaff - but is simply a surcharge that is added to the price of the meal.

Where tipping is common, it may be encouraged as a social convention, but on occasion may actually be vehemently enforced by the restaurant.

Descriptions of Design Activities

At least two views of design activity are consistent with the Action-Centric Perspective. Both involve three basic activities.

In the Reflection-in-Action paradigm, designers alternate between "framing," "making moves," and "evaluate moves". "Framing" refers to conceptualizing the problem, i.e., defining goals and objectives. A "move" is a (tentative) design decision.

In the Sensemaking-Coevolution-Implementation Framework, designers alternate between its three titular activities. Sensemaking includes both framing and evaluating moves. Implementation is the process of constructing the design object. Coevolution is "the process where the design agent simultaneously refines its mental picture of the design object based on its mental picture of the context, and vice versa".

CRITICISM OF THE ACTION-CENTRIC PERSPECTIVE

As this perspective is relatively new, it has not yet encountered much criticism. One possible criticism is that it is less intuitive than The Rational Model.

Design Disciplines

- Applied arts
- Fashion Design
- Graphic Design
- Industrial Design Engineering
- Interior Design
- Product Design
- Instructional Design

Philosophies and Studies of Design

There are countless philosophies for guiding design as the design values and its accompanying aspects within modern design vary, both between different schools of thought and among practicing designers. Design philosophies are usually for determining design goals. A design goal may range from solving the least significant individual problem of the smallest element, to the most holistic influential utopian goals. Design goals are usually for guiding design. However, conflicts over immediate and minor goals may lead to questioning the purpose of design, perhaps to set better long term or ultimate goals.

Philosophies for Guiding Design

Design philosophies are fundamental guiding principles that dictate how a designer approaches his/her practice. Reflections on material culture and environmental concerns (Sustainable design) can guide a design philosophy. One example is the First Things First manifesto which was launched within the graphic design community and states "We propose a reversal of priorities in favor of more useful, lasting and democratic forms of communication-a mindshift away from product marketing and toward the exploration and production of a new kind of meaning. The scope of debate is shrinking; it must expand. Consumerism is running uncontested; it must be challenged by other perspectives expressed, in part, through the visual languages and resources of design."

In *The Sciences of the Artificial* by polymath Herbert Simon the author asserts design to be a meta-discipline of all professions. "Engineers are not the only professional designers. Everyone designs who devises courses of action aimed at changing existing situations into preferred ones. The intellectual activity that produces material artifacts is no different fundamentally from the one that prescribes remedies for a sick patient or the one that devises a new sales plan for a company or a social welfare policy for a state. Design, so construed, is the core of all professional training; it is the principal mark that distinguishes the professions from the sciences. Schools of engineering, as well as schools of architecture, business, education, law, and medicine, are all centrally concerned with the process of design."

Approaches to Design

A design approach is a general philosophy that may or may not include a guide for specific methods. Some are to guide the overall goal of the design. Other approaches are to guide the tendencies of the designer. A combination of approaches may be used if they don't conflict.

Some popular approaches include:

- KISS principle, (Keep it Simple Stupid, etc.), which strives to eliminate unnecessary complications.
- There is more than one way to do it (TIMTOWTDI), a philosophy to allow multiple methods of doing the same thing.
- Use-centered design, which focuses on the goals añd tasks associated with the use of the artifact, rather than focusing on the end user.
- User-centered design, which focuses on the needs, wants, and limitations of the end user of the designed artifact.
- Critical design uses designed artifacts as an embodied critique or commentary on existing values, mores, and practices in a culture.

Methods of Designing

Design Methods is a broad area that focuses on:

- Exploring possibilities and constraints by focusing critical thinking skills to research and define problem spaces for existing products or services— or the creation of new categories;
- Redefining the specifications of design solutions which can lead to better guidelines for traditional design activities (graphic, industrial, architectural, etc.);
- Managing the process of exploring, defining, creating artifacts continually over time;

- Prototyping possible scenarios, or solutions that incrementally or significantly improve the inherited situation;
- Trendspotting; understanding the trend process.

Philosophies for the Purpose of Designs

In philosophy, the abstract noun "design" refers to a pattern with a purpose. Design is thus contrasted with purposelessness, randomness, or lack of complexity.

To study the purpose of designs, beyond individual goals (e.g. marketing, technology, education, entertainment, hobbies), is to question the controversial politics, morals, ethics and needs such as Maslow's hierarchy of needs. "Purpose" may also lead to existential questions such as religious morals and teleology. These philosophies for the "purpose of" designs are in contrast to philosophies for guiding design or methodology.

Often a designer (especially in commercial situations) is not in a position to define purpose. Whether a designer is, is not, or should be concerned with purpose or intended use beyond what they are expressly hired to influence, is debatable, depending on the situation. In society, not understanding or disinterest in the wider role of design might also be attributed to the commissioning agent or client, rather than the designer. Some newer fields of design have built-in purposes and values, such as user-centered design, slow design, and sustainable design.

In structuration theory, achieving consensus and fulfillment of purpose is as continuous as society. Raised levels of achievement often lead to raised expectations. Design is both medium and outcome, generating a Janus-like face, with every ending marking a new beginning.

Design and Art

Today the term design is widely associated with the Applied arts as initiated by Raymond Loewy and teachings at the Bauhaus and Ulm School of Design (HfG Ulm) in Germany during the 20th Century.The boundaries between art and design are blurred, largely due to a range of applications both for the term 'art' and the term 'design'. Applied arts has been used as an umbrella term to define fields of industrial design, graphic design, fashion design, etc.

The term 'decorative arts' is a traditional term used in historical discourses to describe craft objects, and also sits within the umbrella of Applied arts. In graphic arts (2D image making that ranges from photography to illustration) the distinction is often made between fine art and commercial art, based on the context within which the work is produced and how it is traded.

To a degree, some methods for creating work, such as employing intuition, are shared across the disciplines within the Applied arts and Fine art. Mark Getlein suggests the principles of design are "almost instinctive", "built-in", "natural", and part of "our sense of 'rightness'." However, the intended application and context of the resulting works will vary greatly.

The food service equipment for your new café can be conveniently purchased directly from Design & Layout Services. We are a fully authorized commercial kitchen equipment dealer and we purchase your equipment package directly from the manufacturer.

Through volume purchasing power, we are able to offer you competitive pricing on refrigeration, ice machines, ovens, shelving, sinks and display cases. We will consolidate your entire order into a single shipment to be delivered to the job site when your contractor is ready. Many of our design customers take advantage of this one-stop service that saves them valuable time and money.

DESIGN AND ENGINEERING

In engineering, design is a component of the engineering process. Many overlapping methods and processes can be seen when comparing Product design, Industrial design and Engineering. The American Heritage Dictionary defines design as: "To conceive or fashion in the mind; invent," and "To formulate a plan", and defines engineering as: "The application of scientific and mathematical principles to practical ends such as the design, manufacture, and operation of efficient and economical structures, machines, processes, and systems.".

Both are forms of problem-solving with a defined distinction being the application of "scientific and mathematical principles". The increasingly scientific focus of engineering in practice, however, has raised the importance of new more "human-centered" fields of design. How much science is applied in a design is a question of what is considered "science". Along with the question of what is considered science, there is social science versus natural science. Scientists at Xerox PARC made the distinction of design versus engineering at "moving minds" versus "moving atoms".

Jonathan Ive has received several awards for his design of Apple Inc. products like this laptop. In some design fields, personal computers are also used for both design and production

Design and Production

The relationship between design and production is one of planning and executing. In theory, the plan should anticipate and compensate for potential problems in the execution process. Design involves problem-solving and creativity. In contrast, production involves a routine or pre-planned process.

A design may also be a mere plan that does not include a production or engineering process, although a working knowledge of such processes is usually expected of designers. In some cases, it may be unnecessary and/or impractical to expect a designer with a broad multidisciplinary knowledge required for such designs to also have a detailed specialized knowledge of how to produce the product.

Design and production are intertwined in many creative professional careers, meaning problem-solving is part of execution and the reverse. As the cost of rearrangement increases, the need for separating design from production increases as well. For example, a high-budget project, such as a skyscraper, requires separating (design) architecture from (production) construction. A Low-budget project, such as a locally printed office party invitation flyer, can be rearranged and printed dozens of times at the low cost of a few sheets of paper, a few drops of ink, and less than one hour's pay of a desktop publisher.

This is not to say that production never involves problem-solving or creativity, nor that design always involves creativity. Designs are rarely perfect and are sometimes repetitive. The imperfection of a design may task a production position (e.g. production artist, construction worker) with utilizing creativity or problem-solving skills to compensate for what was overlooked in the design process. Likewise, a design may be a simple repetition (copy) of a known preexisting solution, requiring minimal, if any, creativity or problem-solving skills from the designer.

Process Design

"Process design" (in contrast to "design process" mentioned above) refers to the planning of routine steps of a process aside from the expected result. Processes (in general) are treated as a product of design, not the method of design. The term originated with the industrial designing of chemical processes. With the increasing complexities of the information age, consultants and executives have found the term useful to describe the design of business processes as well as manufacturing processes.

Food service Consultants Studio – a certified women-owned, small business – provides commercial and institutional food service professionals and architects innovative solutions to their operational and facility design challenges.

Our consultants are the most credentialed in the industry, reflecting our commitment to design excellence and green initiatives. In addition to facility design, we offer interior design and management advisory services for the culinary arts. Visit our Services page for more information.

In 2011, FCS Principals Doug Huber and Larry Huber received the Top Achiever Award from *Food service Equipment & Supplies* magazine. The award recognizes food service professionals who help raise the industry's overall professionalism through their integrity, customer focus, and ability to build relationships based on honesty and trust with their supply chain partners.

Significance

Because the food service industry in the United States is huge, a lot of people work in food service management. According to the National Restaurant Association, the food service industry is the second-largest private sector employer in the country. It is a "cornerstone of the economy, representing 4 percent of the U.S. gross domestic product and employing 9 percent of the U.S. workforce." Americans spend almost half of their overall food budget in restaurants.

Function

According to the DOL, food service managers oversee the people in the restaurant. They "coordinate activities among various departments, such as kitchen, dining room, and banquet operations." They make sure that the restaurants' employees are working effectively and that the customers are happy. They handle customer complaints about the quality of the food and "ensure that diners are served properly in a timely manner." They also "oversee the inventory and ordering of food, equipment and supplies."

Features

Food service managers have many administrative duties. According to the DOL, they are responsible for interviewing, hiring, training and firing employees. They handle employee payroll information and work records. Food service managers "schedule work hours, making sure that enough workers are present to cover each shift." They also ensure that the restaurant complies with all local liquor laws and sanitation standards.

Types

Larger restaurants and bars have management teams. According to the DOL, these "consist of a general manager, one or more assistant managers, and an executive chef." The general manager is in charge of the restaurant as a whole. The executive chef "is responsible for all food preparation activities, including running kitchen operations, planning menus, and maintaining quality standards for food service." Assistant managers oversee the wait staff and dining area. These divisions are not necessary in smaller restaurants, where one person usually acts as the overall manager.

Considerations

Food service management is a difficult, stressful career. According to the DOL, managers must "be able to fill in for absent workers on short notice." They work extremely long hours: "12 to 15 per day, 50 or more per week, and sometimes 7 days a week." Running a restaurant "can be hectic, and dealing with irate customers or uncooperative employees can be stressful."

Cafeteria

A cafeteria is a type of food service location in which there is little or no waiting staff table service, whether a restaurant or within an institution such as a large office building or school; a school dining location is also referred to as a dining hall or canteen. Cafeterias are different from coffeehouses, although that is the Spanish meaning of the English word.

Instead of table service, there are food-serving counters/stalls, either in a line or allowing arbitrary walking paths. Customers take the food they require as they walk along, placing it on a tray. In addition, there are often stations where customers order food and wait while it is prepared, particularly for items such as hamburgers or tacos which must be served hot and can be quickly prepared.

Alternatively, the patron is given a number and the item is brought to their table. Sometimes, for some food items and drinks, customers collect an empty container, pay at the check-out, and fill the container after the check-out. Free second servings are often allowed under this system. For legal purposes (and the consumption patterns of customers), this system is rarely or never used for alcoholic beverages in the USA.

Customers are either charged a flat rate for admission (as in a buffet), or pay at the check-out for each item.

Some self-service cafeterias charge by the weight of items on a patron's plate.

As cafeterias require few employees, they are often found within a larger institution, catering to the clientele of that institution. For example, schools, colleges and their residence halls, department stores, hospitals, museums, military bases, prisons, and office buildings often have cafeterias.

At one time, upscale cafeteria-style restaurants dominated the culture of the Southern United States, and to a lesser extent the Midwest. There were several prominent chains of them: Bickford's, Morrison's Cafeteria, Piccadilly Cafeteria, S&W Cafeteria, Apple House, K&W, Britling, Wyatt's Cafeteria, and Blue Boar among them. Currently two midwest chains still exist, Sloppy Jo's Luchroom and Manny's, both located in Illinois. There were also a number of smaller chains, usually in and around a single city.

These institutions, with the exception of K&W, went into a decline in the 1960s with the rise of fast food and were largely finished off in the 1980s by the rise of "casual dining". A few chains — notably Luby's and Piccadilly Cafeterias (which took over the Morrison's chain), continue to fill some of the gap left by the decline of the older chains. Many of the smaller Midwestern chains, such as MCL Cafeterias centered around Indianapolis, are still very much in business.

The world's largest non-military cafeteria is in the Brody Complex at Michigan State University. Perhaps the first self-service restaurant (not necessarily cafeteria) in the United States was the Exchange Buffet in New York City, opened September 4, 1885, which catered to an exclusively male clientele. Food was purchased at a counter, and patrons ate standing up. This represents the predecessor of two formats: the cafeteria, described below, and the automat.

During the 1893 World's Columbian Exposition in Chicago, an entrepreneur named John Kruger built an American version of the smörgåsbords he had seen while traveling in Sweden. Emphasizing the simplicity and light fare, he called it the "Cafeteria" - Spanish for "coffee shop". The exposition attracted over 27 million visitors (half the US population at the time) in six months, and it was initially through Kruger's operation that America first heard the term and experienced the self-service dining format.

Meanwhile, in everyday, hometown America, the chain of Childs Restaurants was quickly growing from about 10 locations in New York City (in 1890), to hundreds across the United States and Canada (by 1920). Childs is credited with the critical innovation of adding trays and a "tray line" to the self-service format, which they introduced in 1898 at their 130 Broadway location. Childs did not change its format of sit-down dining, however. This was soon the standard design for most Childs Restaurants - and many imitators - from coast-to-coast, and ultimately the dominant design for cafeterias.

It has also been said that the "cafeteria craze started in May 1905, when a woman named Helen Mosher opened a humble downtown L.A. restaurant where people chose their food at a long counter and carried their own trays to their tables." California does have a long and rich history in the cafeteria format - most notably the many Boos Brothers Cafeterias, and also Clifton's and Schaber's.

However, the facts do not warrant the "wellspring" characterization that some have ascribed to the region. The earliest cafeterias in California were opened at least 12 years after Kruger's Cafeteria, and Childs already had several dozen locations scattered around the country.

Finally, Horn & Hardart, an automat format chain (only slightly different from the cafeteria), was also well established in the mid-Atlantic region before 1900. Between 1960 and 1980, the popularity of cafeteria format restaurants was gradually overcome by the emergence of the fast food restaurant and fast casual restaurant formats.

Other Names

A cafeteria in a U.S. military installation is known as a chow hall, a mess hall, a galley, mess decks or, more formally, a dining facility, whereas in common British Armed Forces parlance, it is known as a cookhouse or mess. Students in the USA often refer to cafeterias as lunchrooms, though breakfast as well as lunch is often eaten there.

Cafeterias serving university dormitories are sometimes called dining halls or dining commons. A food court is a type of cafeteria found in many shopping malls and airports featuring multiple food vendors or concessions, although a food court could equally be styled as a type of restaurant as well, being more aligned with public, rather than institutionalised, dining.

Some monasteries, boarding schools and older universities refer to their cafeteria as a refectory. Modern-day British cathedrals and abbeys, notably in the Church of England, often use the phrase refectory to describe a cafeteria open to the public. Historically, the refectory was generally only used by monks and priests.

For example, although the original 800-year-old refectory at Gloucester Cathedral (the stage setting for dining scenes in the Harry Potter movies) is now mostly used as a choir practice area, the relatively modern 300-year-old extension, now used as a cafeteria by staff and public alike, is today referred to as the refectory.

A cafeteria located in a television studio is often called a commissary. NBC's commissary, The Hungry Peacock, was often joked about by Johnny Carson on The Tonight Show.

COLLEGE CAFETERIA

A college cafeteria is a term in the United States that denotes a cafeteria that is designed to serve college students at the university. In the UK the word *refectory* is often used. Also see the different meanings of the word college around the Anglosphere. These cafeterias can be a part of a residence hall or in a separate building.

Many of these colleges employ their own students to work in the cafeteria. The amount of meals served to students varies from school to school, but is normally around 20 meals per week. Like normal cafeterias, a person will have a tray to select the food that they want, but instead of paying money, they pay beforehand by purchasing a meal plan.

The method of payment for college cafeterias is commonly in the form of a meal plan, whereby the patron pays a certain amount at the start of the semester and the details of the plan are stored on a computer system. Student ID cards are then used to access the meal plan. A meal plan is not necessary to eat at a college cafeteria however.

Meal plans can vary widely in their details to best fit the needs of the students. Typically, the college tracks the student's usage of their plan by counting either the number of pre-defined meal servings, points, dollars, or number of buffet dinners. The plan may give the student a certain number of any of the above per week or semester and they may or may not roll over to the next week or semester.

Many schools offer several different options for using their meal plans. The main cafeteria is usually where most of the meal plan is used but smaller cafeterias, cafés, restaurants, bars, or even fast food chains located on campus may accept meal plans.

A college cafeteria system often has a virtual monopoly on the students due to an isolated location or a requirement that residence contracts include a full meal plan. It is not uncommon for the entire food service operation to be outsourced to a managed services company such as Aramark, Sodexo and Compass Group under the Scolarest name in the United Kingdom.

Hawker Centre

A hawker centre or *food centre* is the name given to open-air complexes in Hong Kong, Malaysia, Singapore and Riau Islands housing many stalls that sell a variety of inexpensive food. They are typically found near public housing estates or transport hubs (such as bus interchanges or train stations).

Hawker centres sprung up in urban areas following the rapid urbanisation in the 1950s and 1960s. In many cases, they were built partly to address the problem of unhygienic food preparation by unlicensed street hawkers. More recently, they have become less ubiquitous due to growing affluence in the urban populations of Malaysia and Singapore. Particularly in Singapore, they are increasingly being replaced by food courts, which are indoor, air conditioned versions of hawker centres located in shopping malls and other commercial venues.

In the 1950s and 1960s, hawker centres were considered to be a venue for the less affluent. They had a reputation for unhygienic food, partly due to the frequent appearance of stray domestic pets and pests. Many hawker centres were poorly managed by their operators, often lacking running water and proper facilities for cleaning.

More recently, hygiene standards have improved, with pressure from the local authorities. This includes the implementation of licensing requirements, where a sufficient standard of hygiene is required for the stall to operate, and rewarding exceptionally good hygiene. Upgrading or reconstruction of hawker centres was initiated in the late 1990s in Singapore. At the same time, hawker centres were renamed food centres.

The hawker centres in Singapore are owned by three government bodies, namely the National Environment Agency (NEA) under the parent Ministry of the Environment and Water Resources (MEWR), Housing and Development Board (HDB) and JTC Corporation. All the centres, in turn, are managed by NEA.

On 5 March 2010, NEA launched www.myhawkers.sg, which is an interactive web portal that offers useful information on hawker centres and food stalls. The portal allows registered users to review or recommend hawker stalls or hawker centres, and also to provide feedback to NEA on hygiene matters in hawker centres.

In Hong Kong, hawker centres are located in market complexes of residential districts. Stalls from hawker centres are converted from Dai Pai Dong by strict regulations and management. The Food and Environmental Hygiene Department manages hawker centres in Hong Kong.

NOTABLE HAWKER CENTRES

The following lists some of the more notable hawker centres in Singapore:

Singapore

- Adam Road Food Centre

- **Alexandra Road Hawker Centre**
- **Amoy Street Food Centre**
- **Bedok Central**
- **Bukit Timah Market and Food Centre**
- **Changi Village Food Centre**
- **Chinatown Complex**
- **Chomp Chomp Food Centre**
- **East Coast Park Food Centre**
- **East Coast Seafood Centre**
- **Geylang Serai Market and Food Centre**
- **Ghim Moh Market and Food Centre**
- **Glutton's Square (defunct)**
- **Golden Mile Food Centre**
- **Golden Shoe Hawker Centre**
- **Hong Lim Complex**
- **Lau Pa Sat**
- **Lavender Food Square**
- **Maxwell Food Centre**
- **Newton Food Centre**
- **Old Airport Cooked Food Centre**
- **People's Park Food Centre**
- **Serangoon Garden Market and Food Centre**
- **Satay Club**
- **Seah Im Food Centre**
- **Shunfu Mart**
- **Tanjong Pagar Plaza**
- **Tekka Centre**
- **Tiong Bahru Food Centre**
- **Whampoa Food Centre**

CHAPTER–2

ARCHITECTURE AND ENGINEERING

Architectural works are often perceived as cultural and political symbols and as works of art. Historical civilizations are often identified with their surviving architectural achievements. Architecture sometimes refers to the activity of designing any kind of system and the term is common in the information technology world.

An architect is a person trained in the planning, design and oversight of the construction of buildings, who practices architecture. To *practice architecture* means to offer or render services in connection with the design and construction of a building, or group of buildings and the space within the site surrounding the buildings,that have as their principal purpose human occupancy or use.

Architecture can mean:

- The art and science of designing and erecting buildings and other physical structures.
- The practice of an architect, where architecture means to offer or render professional services in connection with the design and construction of a building, or group of buildings and the space within the site surrounding the buildings, that have as their principal purpose human occupancy or use.
- A general term to describe buildings and other structures.

- A style and method of design and construction of buildings and other physical structures.

A wider definition may comprise all design activity, from the macro-level (urban design, landscape architecture) to the micro-level (construction details and furniture). Architecture is both the process and product of planning, designing and constructing form, space and ambience that reflect functional, technical, social, and aesthetic considerations. It requires the creative manipulation and coordination of material, technology, light and shadow.

Architecture also encompasses the pragmatic aspects of realizing buildings and structures, including scheduling, cost estimating and construction administration. As documentation produced by architects, typically drawings, plans and technical specifications, architecture defines the structure and/or behavior of a building or any other kind of system that is to be or has been constructed.

Professionally, an architect's decisions affect public safety, and thus an architect must undergo specialized training consisting of advanced education and a *practicum* (or *internship*) for practical experience to earn a license to practice architecture. The practical, technical, and academic requirements for becoming an architect vary by jurisdiction.

The terms architect and architecture are also used in the disciplines of landscape architecture, naval architecture and incorrectly and misleading information technology (for example a software architect). In most of the world's jurisdictions, the professional and commercial uses of the term "architect", outside of the etymological variants noted, with the exception of information technology, is legally protected. It is illegal in the USA for anyone to call themselves an architect or use the title

"Architect" that does not hold a license or registration to practice architecture.

ARCHITECTS IN PRACTICE

The practice of architecture involves offering or rendering services that include pre-design services, programming, planning, providing designs, drawings, specifications and other technical submissions, the administration of construction contracts and the co-ordination of any elements of technical submissions prepared by others (such as by engineers) and technical designers.

Architecture is a business in which technical knowledge, management, and an understanding of business are as important as design. An architect accepts a commission from a client. The commission might involve preparing feasibility reports, building audits, the design of a building or of several buildings, structures, and the spaces among them. The architect participates in developing the requirements the client wants in the building. Throughout the project (planning to occupancy), the architect co-ordinates a design team. Structural, mechanical, and electrical engineers and other specialists, are hired by the client or the architect, who must ensure that the work is co-ordinated to construct the design.

Design Role

The architect hired by a client is responsible for creating a design concept that meets the requirements of that client and provides a facility suitable to the required use. In that, the architect must meet with and question the client [extensively] to ascertain all the requirements and nuances of the planned project. This information, known as a program or brief, is essential to producing a project that meets all the needs and desires of the owner—it is a guide for the architect in creating the design concept.

Architects deal with local and federal jurisdictions about regulations and building codes. The architect might need to comply with local planning and zoning laws, such as required setbacks, height limitations, parking requirements, transparency requirements (windows), and land use. Some established jurisdictions require adherence to design and historic preservation guidelines.

Documentation Role

Architects prepare the technical or "working" documents (construction drawings and specifications), usually coordinated with and supplemented by the work of a variety of disciplines [i.e., with varied expertise like mechanical, plumbing, electrical, civil, structural, etc.] engineers for the building services and that are filed for obtaining permits (development and building permits) that require compliance with building, seismic, and relevant federal and local regulations. These construction drawings and specifications are also used for pricing the work, and for construction.

Construction Role

Architects typically put projects to tender on behalf of their clients, advise on the award of the project to a general contractor, and review the progress of the work during construction. They typically review subcontractor shop drawings and other submittals, prepare and issue site instructions, and provide construction contract administration and Certificates for Payment to the contractor. In many jurisdictions, mandatory certification or assurance of the work is required.

Depending on the client's needs and the jurisdiction's requirements, the spectrum of the architect's services may be extensive (detailed document preparation and construction review) or less inclusive (such as allowing a contractor to exercise considerable design-build functions). With very large, complex projects, an independent construction manager is sometimes hired to assist in design and to manage construction. In the United Kingdom and other countries, a quantity surveyor is often part of the team to provide cost consulting.

ALTERNATE PRACTICE AND SPECIALIZATIONS

Recent decades have seen the rise of specializations within the profession. Many architects and architectural firms focus on certain project types (for example, health care, retail, public housing), technological expertise or project delivery methods. Some architects specialize as building code, building envelope, sustainable design, historic preservation, accessibility and other forms of specialist consultants.

Many architects elect to move into real estate (property) development, corporate facilities planning, project management, construction management, interior design or other related fields.

Professional Requirements

Although there are variations from place to place, in most of the world architects are required to register with the appropriate jurisdiction. To do so, architects are typically required to meet three common requirements: education, experience, and examination.

Educational requirements generally consist of an acredited university degree in architecture. The experience requirement for degreed candidates is usually satisfied by a practicum or internship (usually two to three years, depending on jurisdiction). Finally, a Registration Examination or a series of exams is required prior to licensure.

Professionals engaged in the design and supervision of construction projects prior to the late 19th century were not necessarily trained in a separate architecture program in an academic setting. Instead, they often trained under established architects. Prior to modern times, there was no distinction between architects, engineers and often artists, and the title used varied depending on geographical location.

They often carried the title of master builder, or surveyor, after serving a number of years as an apprentice (such as Sir Christopher Wren). The formal study of architecture in academic institutions played a pivotal role in the development of the profession as a whole, serving as a focal point for advances in architectural technology and theory.

Professional Title Distinctions

According to the American Institute of Architects, titles and job descriptions within American architectural offices might be as follows:

- **Senior Principal/Partner:** Typically an owner or majority shareholder of the firm; may be the founder; titles may include president, chief executive officer, or managing principal/partner.
- **Mid-level Principal/Partner:** Principal or partner; titles may include executive or senior vice president.
- **Junior Principal/Partner:** Recently made a partner or principal of the firm; title may include vice president.
- **Department head/Senior Manager:** Senior management architect or non-registered graduate; responsible for major department(s) or functions; reports to a principal or partner.

- **Project Manager**: Licensed architect, or non-registered graduate with more than 10 years of experience; has overall project management responsibility for a variety of projects or project teams, including client contact, scheduling, and budgeting.
- **Senior Architect/Designer**: Licensed architect, or non-registered graduate with more than 10 years of experience; has a design or technical focus and is responsible for significant project activities.
- **Architect/Designer I**: Recently licensed architect or non-registered graduate with 3–5 years of experience; responsible for particular parts of a project within parameters set by others.
- **Architect/Designer II**: Licensed architect or non-registered graduate with 6–8 years of experience, responsible for daily design or technical development of projects.
- **Architect/Designer III**: Licensed architect or non-registered graduate with 8–10 years of experience; responsible for significant aspects of projects.
- **Intern-Architect**: Unlicensed architecture school graduate participating in defined internship program; develops design or technical solutions under supervision of an architect.

ARCHITECT'S FEES

Architects' fee structures are typically based on a percentage of construction value, hourly rates or a fixed lump sum fee. Combinations of these structures are also common. Fixed fees are usually based on an a project's allocated construction cost and can range between 2 and 12% of new construction cost, depending on a project's size and complexity. Renovation projects typically command higher percentages, as high as 15-20%.

Overall billings for architectural firms range widely, depending on location and economic climate. Billings have traditionally been dependent on the local economic conditions but, with rapid globalization, this is becoming less of a factor for larger international firms. Salaries also vary, depending on experience, position within the firm (staff architect, partner or shareholder, etc.) and the size and location of the firm.

PROFESSIONAL ORGANIZATIONS

Refer to the international list of professional architecture organizations for groups created to promote career and business development in architecture. A wide variety of prizes are awarded to architects to acknowledge superior buildings, structures and professional careers.

Prizes, Awards and Titles

The most lucrative award an architect can receive is the Pritzker Prize, sometimes termed the "Nobel Prize for architecture." Other prestigious architectural awards are the Aga Khan Award for Architecture, the Richard H. Driehaus Prize for Classical Architecture, the Alvar Aalto Medal (Finland), the Carlsberg Architecture Prize (Denmark), and the Governor General's Awards (Canada). Other awards for excellence in architecture are given by national professional associations such as the American Institute of Architects (AIA), the Royal Institute of British Architects (RIBA), and the Royal Architectural Institute of Canada (RAIC).

Architects in the UK who have made contributions to the profession through design excellence or architectural education, or have in some other way advanced the profession, are elected Fellows of the Royal Institute of

British Architects and can write FRIBA after their name if they feel so inclined. Architects in the USA who have made contributions to the profession through design excellence or architectural education, or have in some other way advanced the profession, are elected Fellows of the American Institute of Architects and can write FAIA after their name. Architects in Canada who have made outstanding contributions to the profession through contribution to research, scholarship, public service or professional standing to the good of architecture in Canada, or elsewhere, may be recognized as a Fellow of the Royal Architectural Institute of Canada and can write FRAIC after their name.

Architectural Designer

An architectural designer is an architect that is primarily involved in the design of buildings or urban landscapes, as opposed to the construction documents and management required to construct it. Architectural designers have good creative skills, imagination and artistic talent. Although most students of architecture are trained to be designers in school, not all become designers in practice. Non-registered designers are similar, but cannot legally refer to themselves as "architectural" designers in most parts of the world. Most are referred to as building designers, especially when not employed by an architectural firm.

Many large architectural firms have architectural designers that set what the general public views as the "style" of the firm's projects. These firms may actually have groups of designers (design studios), often divided into their own separate niche markets (education, healthcare, housing, etc.) In smaller architectural firms, the architectural designers tend to remain involved with the project right through completion, and actually take an active role in documentation and management, sometimes to the point of supervising construction. It is worth noting that most "star" architects, that have become household names, are known because of their skill as architectural designers.

Architectural Theory

Architectural theory is the act of thinking, discussing, or most importantly writing about architecture. Architectural theory is taught in most architecture schools and is practiced by the world's leading architects. Some forms that architecture theory takes are the lecture or dialogue, the treatise or book, and the paper project or competition entry.

Architectural theory is often didactic, and theorists tend to stay close to or work from within schools. It has existed in some form since antiquity, and as publishing became more common, architectural theory gained an increased richness. Books, magazines, and journals published an unprecedented amount of works by architects and critics in the 20th century.

As a result, styles and movements formed and dissolved much more quickly than the relatively enduring modes in earlier history. It is to be expected that the use of the internet will further the discourse on architecture in the 21st century.

Antiquity

There is little information or evidence about major architectural theory in antiquity, until the 1st century BCE, with the work of Vitruvius. This does not mean, however, that such works did not exist. Many works never survived antiquity, and the burning of the Alexandria Library shows us a very good example of this.

Vitruvius was a Roman writer, architect, and engineer active in the 1st century BCE. He was the most prominent architectural theorist in the Roman Empire known today, having written *De architectura*, (known today as *The Ten Books of Architecture*), a treatise written of Latin and Ancient Greek/Greek on architecture, dedicated to the emperor Augustus. It is the only surviving major book on architecture from classical antiquity.

Probably written between 27 and 23 BCE, it is the only contemporary source on classical architecture to have survived. Divided into ten sections or "books", it covers almost every aspect of Roman architecture, from town planning, materials, decorations, temples, water supplies, etc. The famous orders of architecture that we can see in every classical architecture are rigorously defined in the books.

It also gathers three fundamental laws that Architecture must obey, in order to be so considered: *firmitas, utilitas, venustas*: firmness, commodity (in the sense of functionality), and delight. The rediscovery of Vitruvius' work had a profound influence on architects of the Renaissance, prompting the rise of the Renaissance style. Renaissance architects, such as Niccoli, Brunelleschi and Leon Battista Alberti, found in "De Architectura" their rationale for raising their branch of knowledge to a scientific discipline.

Middle Ages

Throughout the Middle Ages, architectural knowledge was passed by transcription, word of mouth and technically in master builders' lodges. Due to the laborious nature of transcription, few examples of architectural theory were penned in this time period. Most works that from this period were theological, and were transcriptions of the bible, so the architectural theories were the notes on structures included therein. The Abbot Suger's Liber de rebus in administratione sua gestis, was an architectural document that emerged with gothic architecture. Another was Villard de Honnecourt's portfolio of drawings from about the 1230s.

In Song Dynasty China, Li Jie published the *Yingzao Fashi* in 1103, which was an architectural treatise that codified elements of Chinese architecture.

Renaissance

The first great work of architectural theory of this period belongs to Leon Battista Alberti, *De Re Aedificatoria*, which placed Vitruvius at the core of the most profound theoretical tradition of the modern ages. From Alberti, good architecture is validated through the Vitruvian triad, which defines its purpose. This triplet conserved all its validity until the 19th century.

Enlightenment

The Age of the Enlightenment witnessed considerable development in architectural theory on the European continent. New archeological discoveries (such as those of Pompeii and Herculaneum) drove new interest in Classical art and architecture. Thus the term Neoclassicism (exemplified by the writings of Prussian art critic Johann Joachim Winkelmann) arose to designate 18th-century architecture which looked to these new Classical precedents for inspiration in building design.

Major architectural theorists of the Enlightenment include Julien-David Leroy, Abbé Marc-Antoine Laugier, Giovanni Battista Piranesi, Robert Adam, James Stuart, and Nicholas Revett. Georg Friedrich Hegel also had a significant impact on architectural theory.

Nineteenth Century

A vibrant strain of Neoclassicism, inherited from Marc-Antoine Laugier's seminal Essai, provided the foundation for two generations of international activity around the core themes of classicism, primitivism and a "return to Nature."

Reaction against the dominance of neo-classical architecture came to the fore in the 1820s with Augustus Pugin providing a moral and theoretical basis for Gothic Revival architecture, and in the 1840s John Ruskin developed this ethos.

The American sculptor Horatio Greenough published the essay *American Architecture* in August 1843 in which he rejected the imitation of old styles of buildings and outlined the functional relationship between architecture and decoration. These theories anticipated the development of Functionalism in modern architecture.

Towards the end of the century, there occurred a blossoming of theoretical activity. In England, Ruskin's ideals underpinned the emergence of the Arts and Crafts movement exemplified by the writings of William Morris. This in turn formed the basis for Art Nouveau in the UK, exemplified by the work of Charles Rennie Mackintosh, and influenced the Vienna Secession.

On the Continent, the theories of Viollet-le-Duc and Gottfried Semper provided the springboard for enormous vitality of thought dedicated to architectural innovation and the renovation of the notion of style. Semper in particular developed an international following, in Germany, England, Switzerland, Austria, Bohemia, France, Italy and the United States.

The generation born during the middle-third of the 19th century was largely enthralled with the opportunities presented by Semper's combination of a breathtaking historical scope and a methodological granularity. In contrast to more recent, and thus "modern", thematically self-organized theoretical activities, this generation did not coalesce into a "movement."

They did, however, seem to converge on Semper's use of the concept of *Realismus*, and they are thus labelled proponents of architectural realism. Among the most active Architectural Realists were: Georg Heuser, Rudolf Redtenbacher, Constantin Lipsius, Hans Auer, Paul Sédille, Lawrence Harvey, Otto Wagner and Richard Streiter.

Twentieth Century

Around the turn of the 20th century Camillo Sitte published the *City Planning According to Artistic Principles* which was not exactly a criticism of architectural form, but more precisely an aesthetic criticism of the 19th century's urbanism. Mainly an urban planning theory book, it has a deep influence in architecture, as the two disciplines are deeply intertwined. It was also highly successful in its time.

Between 1889 and 1922 it is edited five times, French translation came in 1902 and the English translation in 1945, in New York. For Sitte, the most important is not the architectural shape or form of each building, but the inherent creative quality of urban space, the whole as much more than the sum of its parts.

Modernist movements rejected these thoughts and Le Corbusier energetically dismissed the work. Nevertheless, his work is often used and cited as a criticism to the Modernist movement, and reemerged its importance in the post-modernist movement, late in the sixties. Also on the topic of artistic notions with regard to urbanism was Louis Sullivan's *The Tall Office Building Artistically Considered* of 1896. In this essay, Sullivan penned his famous adage "form forever follows function"; a phrase that was to be later adopted as a central tenet of Modernist architectural theory.

While later architects adopted the abbreviated phrase "form follows function" as a polemic in service of functionalist doctrine, Sullivan wrote of function with regard to biological functions of the natural order. Another influential planning theorist of this time was Ebenezer Howard, who founded the garden city movement. This movement formed communities with architecture in the Arts and Crafts style at Letchworth and Welwyn Garden City and popularised the style as domestic architecture.

In Vienna, modernism had many theorists and proponents. An early use of the term "modern architecture" in print, was in the title of a book by Otto Wagner, who gave examples of his own work representative of the Vienna Secession with art nouveau illustrations, and didactic teachings to his students. Soon thereafter, Adolf Loos wrote *Ornament and Crime*, and while his own style can be seen as part of the transition to Art Deco, his demand for "the elimination of ornament" joined the slogan "form follows function" as a principle of the modern architecture movement which came to dominate the 20th Century.

Walter Gropius, Ludwig Mies van der Rohe and Le Corbusier provided the theoretical basis for the international style with aims of using industrialised architecture to reshape society. Frank Lloyd Wright, while modernist in rejecting historic revivalism, was idiosyncratic in his theory, which he conveyed in copious writing. Wright did not subscribe to the tenets of the International Style, but evolved what he hoped would be an American, in contrast to a European, progressive course.

Wright's style, however, was highly personal, involving his private views of man and nature. He created no major "school" or theoretical movement. Wright was more poetic and firmly maintained the 19th century view of the creative artist as unique genius. This limited the relevance of his theoretical propositions. Towards the end of the century postmodern architecture reacted against the austerity of High Modern (International Style) principles, viewed as narrowly normative and doctrinaire.

Contemporary

In contemporary architectural discourse theory has become more concerned with its position within culture generally, which is why university courses on architecture theory may often spend just as much time discussing philosophy and cultural studies as buildings. The notion that theory also entailed critique stemmed from post-structural literary studies. This, however, pushed architecture towards the notion of avant-gardism for its own sake - in many ways repeating the 19th century 'art for art's sake' outlook.

Since 2000 this has materialised in architecture through concerns with the rapid rise of urbanism and globalization, but also a pragmatic understanding that the city can no longer be a homogenous totality. Interests in fragmentation and architecture as transient objects further such thinking (e.g. the concern for employing high technology). And yet this can also be tied into general concerns such as ecology, mass media, and economism.

In the past decade, there has been a resurgence of the old "organic design" theories, but in a much more scientific setting. Several currents and design methodologies are being developed simultaneously, and some of these reinforce whereas others contrast with each other. One of these trends is Biomimicry, which is the explicit copying of forms and structures found in biological organisms for buildings. Architects design organic-looking buildings in the belief that by copying nature, Organic architecture reaches a more attractive form.

Another trend is the exploration of computational techniques, which are strongly influenced by algorithms relevant to biological processes. Trying to utilize Computational creativity in architecture, Genetic algorithms developed in computer science are applied to evolve designs on a computer, and some of these are proposed and built as actual structures. There exists, however, a controversy as to whether all such evolved designs through Design computing are truly appropriate for buildings, or are merely attractive forms that may be too complex for habitation.

The new discipline of Biophilia developed by E. O. Wilson suggests the advantages of forms inspired by biological structures, but in a more profound way than simple mimicry. Wilson's original idea is extended by Stephen R. Kellert in the Biophilia hypothesis, and applied to architectural design in the book "Biophilic Design".

Mathematical features of biological forms such as fractals, Scale-invariance, very sophisticated notions of symmetry, Self-similarity, and complex Hierarchy are proposed as essential tools for designing architectural forms. Trying to understand the complex interaction between humans and their environment gained from Human-computer interaction, Mobile robotics, and Artificial intelligence leads to ideas in Intelligence-Based Design.

We are witnessing a growth of new ideas that are generating an entirely new type of architectural theory. It bears little resemblance to the dominant school of architectural theory based on linguistic analysis, philosophy, post-structuralism, or cultural theory.

Engineering

Engineering is the discipline, art, and profession of acquiring and applying scientific, mathematical, economic, social, and practical knowledge to design and build structures, machines, devices, systems, materials and processes that safely realize improvements to the lives of people.

The American Engineers' Council for Professional Development (ECPD, the predecessor of ABET) has defined "engineering" as:

The creative application of scientific principles to design or develop structures, machines, apparatus, or manufacturing processes, or works utilizing them singly or in combination; or to construct or operate the same with full cognizance of their design; or to forecast their behavior under specific operating conditions; all as respects an intended function, economics of operation and safety to life and property.

One who practices engineering is called an engineer, and those licensed to do so may have more formal designations such as Professional Engineer, Chartered Engineer, Incorporated Engineer, Ingenieur or European Engineer. The broad discipline of engineering encompasses a range of more specialized subdisciplines, each with a more specific emphasis on certain fields of application and particular areas of technology.

The *concept* of engineering has existed since ancient times as humans devised fundamental inventions such as the pulley, lever, and wheel. Each of these inventions is consistent with the modern definition of engineering, exploiting basic mechanical principles to develop useful tools and objects.

The term *engineering* itself has a much more recent etymology, deriving from the word *engineer*, which itself dates back to 1325, when an *engine'er* (literally, one who operates an *engine*) originally referred to "a constructor of military engines." In this context, now obsolete, an "engine" referred to a military machine, *i.e.*, a mechanical contraption used in war (for example, a catapult). Notable exceptions of the obsolete usage which have survived to the present day are military engineering corps, *e.g.*, the U.S. Army Corps of Engineers.

The word "engine" itself is of even older origin, ultimately deriving from the Latin *ingenium* (c. 1250), meaning "innate quality, especially mental power, hence a clever invention."

Later, as the design of civilian structures such as bridges and buildings matured as a technical discipline, the term civil engineering entered the lexicon as a way to distinguish between those specializing in the construction of such non-military projects and those involved in the older discipline of military engineering.

Ancient Era

The Pharos of Alexandria, the pyramids in Egypt, the Hanging Gardens of Babylon, the Acropolis and the Parthenon in Greece, the Roman aqueducts, Via Appia and the Colosseum, Teotihuacán and the cities and pyramids of the Mayan, Inca and Aztec Empires, the Great Wall of China, among many others, stand as a testament to the ingenuity and skill of the ancient civil and military engineers.

The earliest civil engineer known by name is Imhotep. As one of the officials of the Pharaoh, Djosèr, he probably designed and supervised the construction of the Pyramid of Djoser (the Step Pyramid) at Saqqara in Egypt around 2630-2611 BC. He may also have been responsible for the first known use of columns in architecture.

Ancient Greece developed machines in both the civilian and military domains. The Antikythera mechanism, the first known mechanical computer, and the mechanical inventions of Archimedes are examples of early mechanical engineering. Some of Archimedes' inventions as well as the Antikythera mechanism required sophisticated knowledge of differential gearing or epicyclic gearing, two key principles in machine theory that helped design the gear trains of the Industrial revolution, and are still widely used today in diverse fields such as robotics and automotive engineering.

Chinese, Greek and Roman armies employed complex military machines and inventions such as artillery which was developed by the Greeks around the 4th century B.C., the trireme, the ballista and the catapult. In the Middle Ages, the Trebuchet was developed.

Renaissance Era

The first electrical engineer is considered to be William Gilbert, with his 1600 publication of De Magnete, who was the originator of the term "electricity".

The first steam engine was built in 1698 by mechanical engineer Thomas Savery. The development of this device gave rise to the industrial revolution in the coming decades, allowing for the beginnings of mass production.

With the rise of engineering as a profession in the eighteenth century, the term became more narrowly applied to fields in which mathematics and science were applied to these ends. Similarly, in addition to military and civil engineering the fields then known as the mechanic arts became incorporated into engineering.

Modern Era

Electrical engineering can trace its origins in the experiments of Alessandro Volta in the 1800s, the experiments of Michael Faraday, Georg Ohm and others and the invention of the electric motor in 1872. The work of James Maxwell and Heinrich Hertz in the late 19th century gave rise to the field of Electronics. The later inventions of the vacuum tube and the transistor further accelerated the development of electronics to such an extent that electrical and electronics engineers currently outnumber their colleagues of any other Engineering specialty.

The inventions of Thomas Savery and the Scottish engineer James Watt gave rise to modern Mechanical Engineering. The development of specialized machines and their maintenance tools during the industrial revolution led to the rapid growth of Mechanical Engineering both in its birthplace Britain and abroad.

Chemical Engineering, like its counterpart Mechanical Engineering, developed in the nineteenth century during the Industrial Revolution. Industrial scale manufacturing demanded new materials and new processes and by 1880 the need for large scale production of chemicals was such that a new industry was created, dedicated to the development and large scale manufacturing of chemicals in new industrial plants. The role of the chemical engineer was the design of these chemical plants and processes.

Aeronautical Engineering deals with aircraft design while Aerospace Engineering is a more modern term that expands the reach envelope of the discipline by including spacecraft design. Its origins can be traced back to the aviation pioneers around the turn of the century from the 19th century to the 20th although the work of Sir George Cayley has recently been dated as being from the last decade of the 18th century. Early knowledge of aeronautical engineering was largely empirical with some concepts and skills imported from other branches of engineering.

The first PhD in engineering (technically, *applied science and engineering*) awarded in the United States went to Willard Gibbs at Yale University in 1863; it was also the second PhD awarded in science in the U.S.

Only a decade after the successful flights by the Wright brothers, the 1920s saw extensive development of aeronautical engineering through development of World War I military aircraft. Meanwhile, research to provide fundamental background science continued by combining theoretical physics with experiments. In 1990, with the rise of computer technology, the first search engine was built by computer engineer Alan Emtage.

MAIN BRANCHES OF ENGINEERING

Engineering, much like other science, is a broad discipline which is often broken down into several sub-disciplines. These disciplines concern themselves with differing areas of engineering work. Although initially an engineer will usually be trained in a specific discipline, throughout an engineer's career the engineer may become multi-disciplined, having worked in several of the outlined areas. Engineering is often characterized as having four main branches:

- Chemical engineering – The exploitation of chemical principles in order to carry out large scale chemical process, as well as designing new specialty materials and fuels.
- Civil engineering – The design and construction of public and private works, such as infrastructure (roads, railways, water supply and treatment etc.), bridges and buildings.
- Electrical engineering – a very broad area that may encompass the design and study of various electrical & electronic systems, such as electrical circuits, generators, motors, electromagnetic/ electromechanical devices, electronic devices, electronic circuits, optical fibers, optoelectronic devices, computer systems, telecommunications and electronics.
- Mechanical engineering – The design of physical or mechanical systems, such as power and energy systems, aerospace/aircraft products, weapon systems, transportation products engines, compressors, powertrains, kinematic chains, vacuum technology, and vibration isolation equipment.

Beyond these four, sources vary on other main branches. Historically, naval engineering and mining engineering were major branches. Modern fields sometimes included as major branches include aerospace, architectural, biomedical, industrial and nuclear engineering.

New specialties sometimes combine with the traditional fields and form new branches. A new or emerging area of application will commonly be defined temporarily as a permutation or subset of existing disciplines; there is often gray area as to when a given sub-field becomes large and/or prominent enough to warrant classification as a new "branch." One key indicator of such emergence is when major universities start establishing departments and programs in the new field.For each of these fields there exists considerable overlap, especially in the areas of the application of sciences to their disciplines such as physics, chemistry and mathematics.

Methodology

Engineers apply the sciences of physics and mathematics to find suitable solutions to problems or to make improvements to the status quo. More than ever, engineers are now required to have knowledge of relevant sciences for their design projects, as a result, they keep on learning new material throughout their career.

If multiple options exist, engineers weigh different design choices on their merits and choose the solution that best matches the requirements. The crucial and unique task of the engineer is to identify, understand, and interpret the constraints on a design in order to produce a successful result. It is usually not enough to build a technically successful product; it must also meet further requirements.

Constraints may include available resources, physical, imaginative or technical limitations, flexibility for future modifications and additions, and other factors, such as requirements for cost, safety, marketability, productibility, and serviceability. By understanding the constraints, engineers derive specifications for the limits within which a viable object or system may be produced and operated.

Problem Solving

Engineers use their knowledge of science, mathematics, logic, economics, and appropriate experience or tacit knowledge to find suitable solutions to a problem. Creating an appropriate mathematical model of a problem allows them to analyze it (sometimes definitively), and to test potential solutions.

Usually multiple reasonable solutions exist, so engineers must evaluate the different design choices on their merits and choose the solution that best meets their requirements. Genrich Altshuller, after gathering statistics on a large number of patents, suggested that compromises are at the heart of "low-level" engineering designs, while at a higher level the best design is one which eliminates the core contradiction causing the problem.

Engineers typically attempt to predict how well their designs will perform to their specifications prior to full-scale production. They use, among other things: prototypes, scale models, simulations, destructive tests, nondestructive tests, and stress tests. Testing ensures that products will perform as expected.

Engineers as professionals take seriously their responsibility to produce designs that will perform as expected and will not cause unintended harm to the public at large. Engineers typically include a factor of safety in their designs to reduce the risk of unexpected failure. However, the greater the safety factor, the less efficient the design may be.

The study of failed products is known as forensic engineering, and can help the product designer in evaluating his or her design in the light of real conditions. The discipline is of greatest value after disasters, such as bridge collapses, when careful analysis is needed to establish the cause or causes of the failure.

Computer Use

As with all modern scientific and technological endeavors, computers and software play an increasingly important role. As well as the typical business application software there are a number of computer aided applications (Computer-aided technologies) specifically for engineering. Computers can be used to generate models of fundamental physical processes, which can be solved using numerical methods.

One of the most widely used tools in the profession is computer-aided design (CAD) software which enables engineers to create 3D models, 2D drawings, and schematics of their designs. CAD together with Digital mockup (DMU) and CAE software such as finite element method analysis or analytic element method allows engineers to create models of designs that can be analyzed without having to make expensive and time-consuming physical prototypes.

These allow products and components to be checked for flaws; assess fit and assembly; study ergonomics; and to analyze static and dynamic characteristics of systems such as stresses, temperatures, electromagnetic emissions, electrical currents and voltages, digital logic levels, fluid flows, and kinematics. Access and distribution of all this information is generally organized with the use of Product Data Management software.

There are also many tools to support specific engineering tasks such as Computer-aided manufacture (CAM) software to generate CNC machining instructions; Manufacturing Process Management software for production engineering; EDA for printed circuit board (PCB) and circuit schematics for electronic engineers; MRO applications for maintenance management; and AEC software for civil engineering.

In recent years the use of computer software to aid the development of goods has collectively come to be known as Product Lifecycle Management (PLM).

Social Context

Engineering is a subject that ranges from large collaborations to small individual projects. Almost all engineering projects are beholden to some sort of financing agency: a company, a set of investors, or a government. The few types of engineering that are minimally constrained by such issues are pro bono engineering and open design engineering.

By its very nature engineering is bound up with society and human behavior. Every product or construction used by modern society will have been influenced by engineering design. Engineering design is a very powerful tool to make changes to environment, society and economies, and its application brings with it a great responsibility. Many engineering societies have established codes of practice and codes of ethics to guide members and inform the public at large.

Engineering projects can be subject to controversy. Examples from different engineering disciplines include the development of nuclear weapons, the Three Gorges Dam, the design and use of Sport utility vehicles and the extraction of oil. In response, some western engineering companies have enacted serious corporate and social responsibility policies.

Engineering is a key driver of human development. Sub-Saharan Africa in particular has a very small engineering capacity which results in many African nations being unable to develop crucial infrastructure without outside aid. The attainment of many of the Millennium Development Goals requires the achievement of sufficient engineering capacity to develop infrastructure and sustainable technological development.

All overseas development and relief NGOs make considerable use of engineers to apply solutions in disaster and development scenarios. A number of charitable organizations aim to use engineering directly for the good of mankind:

RELATIONSHIPS WITH OTHER DISCIPLINES

There exists an overlap between the sciences and engineering practice; in engineering, one applies science. Both areas of endeavor rely on accurate observation of materials and phenomena. Both use mathematics and classification criteria to analyze and communicate observations.

Scientists are expected to interpret their observations and to make expert recommendations for practical action based on those interpretations. Scientists may also have to complete engineering tasks, such as designing experimental apparatus or building prototypes. Conversely, in the process of developing technology engineers sometimes find themselves exploring new phenomena, thus becoming, for the moment, scientists.

In the book What Engineers Know and How They Know It, Walter Vincenti asserts that engineering research has a character different from that of scientific research. First, it often deals with areas in which the basic physics and/or chemistry are well understood, but the problems themselves are too complex to solve in an exact manner.

Examples are the use of numerical approximations to the Navier-Stokes equations to describe aerodynamic flow over an aircraft, or the use of Miner's rule to calculate fatigue damage. Second, engineering research employs many semi-empirical methods that are foreign to pure scientific research, one example being the method of parameter variation.

As stated by Fung et al. in the revision to the classic engineering text, Foundations of Solid Mechanics:

"Engineering is quite different from science. Scientists try to understand nature. Engineers try to make things that do not exist in nature. Engineers stress invention. To embody an invention the engineer must put his idea in concrete terms, and design something that people can use. That something can be a device, a gadget, a material, a method, a computing program, an innovative experiment, a new solution to a problem, or an improvement on what is existing.

Since a design has to be concrete, it must have its geometry, dimensions, and characteristic numbers. Almost all engineers working on new designs find that they do not have all the needed information. Most often, they are limited by insufficient scientific knowledge. Thus they study mathematics, physics, chemistry, biology and mechanics. Often they have to add to the sciences relevant to their profession. Thus engineering sciences are born."

Although engineering solutions make use of scientific principles, engineers must also take into account safety, efficiency, economy, reliability and constructibility or ease of fabrication, as well as legal considerations such as patent infringement or liability in the case of failure of the solution.

Medicine and Biology

The study of the human body, albeit from different directions and for different purposes, is an important common link between medicine and some engineering disciplines. Medicine aims to sustain, enhance and even replace functions of the human body, if necessary, through the use of technology.

Modern medicine can replace several of the body's functions through the use of artificial organs and can significantly alter the function of the human body through artificial devices such as, for example, brain implants and pacemakers. The fields of Bionics and medical Bionics are dedicated to the study of synthetic implants pertaining to natural systems.

Conversely, some engineering disciplines view the human body as a biological machine worth studying, and are dedicated to emulating many of its functions by replacing biology with technology. This has led to fields such as artificial intelligence, neural networks, fuzzy logic, and robotics. There are also substantial interdisciplinary interactions between engineering and medicine.

Both fields provide solutions to real world problems. This often requires moving forward before phenomena are completely understood in a more rigorous scientific sense and therefore experimentation and empirical knowledge is an integral part of both.

Medicine, in part, studies the function of the human body. The human body, as a biological machine, has many functions that can be modeled using Engineering methods.

The heart for example functions much like a pump, the skeleton is like a linked structure with levers, the brain produces electrical signals etc. These similarities as well as the increasing importance and application of Engineering principles in Medicine, led to the development of the field of biomedical engineering that uses concepts developed in both disciplines.

Newly emerging branches of science, such as Systems biology, are adapting analytical tools traditionally used for engineering, such as systems modeling and computational analysis, to the description of biological systems.

Art

There are connections between engineering and art; they are direct in some fields, for example, architecture, landscape architecture and industrial design (even to the extent that these disciplines may sometimes be included in a University's Faculty of Engineering); and indirect in others.

The Art Institute of Chicago, for instance, held an exhibition about the art of NASA's aerospace design. Robert Maillart's bridge design is perceived by some to have been deliberately artistic. At the University of South Florida, an engineering professor, through a grant with the National Science Foundation, has developed a course that connects art and engineering.

Among famous historical figures Leonardo Da Vinci is a well known Renaissance artist and engineer, and a prime example of the nexus between art and engineering.

Other Fields

In Political science the term engineering has been borrowed for the study of the subjects of Social engineering and Political engineering, which deal with forming political and social structures using engineering methodology coupled with political science principles. Financial engineering has similarly borrowed the term.

Chapter–3

Fine Dining and Quick Service

Dining in is a formal military ceremony for members of a company or other unit, which includes a dinner, drinking, and other events to foster camaraderie and esprit de corps.

The United States Army, the United States Navy the United States Coast Guard and the United States Air Force refer to this event as a dining in or dining-in The United States Marine Corps refers to it as mess night. Other names include regimental dinner, guest night, formal mess dinner, and band night.

The dining in is a formal event for all unit members, male and female; though some specialized mess nights can be officer- or enlisted-only. The unit chaplain is usually also invited, if an invocation is needed. A unit's dining-in consists of only the members of the unit, with the possible exception of the guest(s) of honor. An optional formal dinner, known as the dining-out may include spouses and other guests. The dining-out follows the same basic rules of the dining-in, but is often tailored to minimize some of the military traditions and be more interesting to civilian guests.

"Except for the annual celebration of the Marine Corps Birthday, no social function associated with the smaller of America's naval services is more enjoyed, admired and imitated than the mess night."

A fast food restaurant, sometimes known as a quick service restaurant or QSR, is a specific type of restaurant characterized both by its fast food cuisine and by minimal table service. Food served in fast food restaurants typically caters to a "meat-sweet diet" and is offered from a limited menu; is cooked in bulk in advance and kept hot; is finished and packaged to order; and is usually available ready to take away, though seating may be provided.

Fast food restaurants are usually part of a restaurant chain or franchise operation, which provisions standardized ingredients and/or partially prepared foods and supplies to each restaurant through controlled supply channels. The term "fast food" was recognized in a dictionary by Merriam-Webster in 1951.

Arguably the first fast food restaurants originated in the United States with White Castle in 1916. Today, American-founded fast food chains such as McDonald's and KFC are multinational corporations with outlets across the globe.

Variations on the fast food restaurant concept include fast casual restaurants and catering trucks. Fast casual restaurants have higher sit-in ratios, and customers can sit and have their orders brought to them. Catering trucks often park just outside worksites and are popular with factory workers.

Some trace the modern history of fast food in America to July 7, 1912, with the opening of a fast food restaurant called the Automat in New York. The Automat was a cafeteria with its prepared foods behind small glass windows and coin-operated slots. Joseph Horn and Frank Hardart had already opened the first Horn & Hardart Automat in Philadelphia in 1902, but their "Automat" at Broadway and 13th Street, in New York City, created a sensation. Numerous Automat restaurants were built around the country to deal with the demand. Automats remained extremely popular throughout the 1920s and 1930s.

The company also popularized the notion of "take-out" food, with their slogan "Less work for Mother". The American company White Castle is generally credited with opening the second fast-food outlet in Wichita, Kansas in 1921, selling hamburgers for five cents from its inception and spawned numerous competitors. It is arguable because most historians and Secondary School textbooks state that A&W was the first fast food restaurant, which opened in 1919.(E. Tavares)

The hamburger restaurant concept which is most associated with the term "fast food" was created by two brothers originally from Nashua, New Hampshire. Richard (Dick) and Maurice (Mac) McDonald opened a barbecue drive-in in 1940 in the city of San Bernardino, California. After discovering that most of their profits came from hamburgers, the brothers closed their restaurant for three months and reopened it in 1948 as a walk-up stand offering a simple menu of hamburgers, french fries, shakes, coffee, and Coca-Cola, served in disposable paper wrapping.

As a result, they were able to produce hamburgers and fries constantly, without waiting for customer orders, and could serve them immediately; hamburgers cost 15 cents, about half the price at a typical diner. Their streamlined production method, which they named the "Speedee Service System" was influenced by the production line innovations of Henry Ford.

By 1954, The McDonald brothers' stand was restaurant equipment manufacturer Prince Castle's biggest purchaser of milkshake blending machines. Prince Castle salesman Ray Kroc traveled to California to discover why the company had purchased almost a dozen of the units as opposed to the normal one or two found in most restaurants of the time. Enticed by the success of the McDonald's concept, Kroc signed a franchise agreement with the brothers and began opening McDonald's restaurants in Illinois.

By 1961, Kroc had bought out the brothers and created what is now the modern McDonald's Corporation. One of the major parts of his business plan was to promote cleanliness of his restaurants to growing groups of Americans that had become aware of food safety issues. As part of his commitment to cleanliness, Kroc often took part in cleaning his own Des Plaines, Illinois outlet by hosing down the garbage cans and scraping gum off the cement. Another concept Kroc added was great swaths of glass which enabled the customer to view the food preparation, a practice still found in chains such as Krispy Kreme. A clean atmosphere was only part of Kroc's grander plan which separated McDonald's from the rest of the competition and attributes to their great success. Kroc envisioned making his restaurants appeal to suburban families.

At roughly the same time as Kroc was conceiving what eventually became McDonald's Corporation, two Miami, Florida businessmen, James McLamore and David Edgerton, opened a franchise of the predecessor to what is now the international fast food restaurant chain Burger King. McLamore had visited the original McDonald's hamburger stand belonging to the McDonald brothers; sensing potential in their innovative assembly line-based production system, he decided he wanted to open a similar operation of his own.

The two partners eventually decided to invest their money in Jacksonville, Florida-based Insta-Burger King. Originally opened in 1953, the founders and owners of the chain, Kieth J. Kramer and his wife's uncle Matthew

Burns, opened their first stores around a piece of equipment known as the Insta-Broiler. The Insta-Broiler oven proved so successful at cooking burgers, they required all of their franchises to carry the device.

By 1959 McLamore and Edgarton were operating several locations within the Miami-Dade area and were growing at a fast clip. Despite the success of their operation, the partners discovered that the design of the insta-broiler made the unit's heating elements prone to degradation from the drippings of the beef patties. The pair eventually created a mechanized gas grill that avoided the problems by changing the way the meat patties were cooked in the unit. After the original company began to falter in 1959, it was purchased by McLamore and Edgerton who renamed the company Burger King.

While fast food restaurants usually have a seating area in which customers can eat the food on the premises, orders are designed to be taken away, and traditional table service is rare. Orders are generally taken and paid for at a wide counter, with the customer waiting by the counter for a tray or container for their food. A "drive-through" service can allow customers to order and pick up food from their cars.

Nearly from its inception, fast food has been designed to be eaten "on the go" and often does not require traditional cutlery and is eaten as a finger food. Common menu items at fast food outlets include fish and chips, sandwiches, pitas, hamburgers, fried chicken, french fries, chicken nuggets, tacos, pizza, and ice cream, although many fast food restaurants offer "slower" foods like chili, mashed potatoes, and salads.

Cuisine

Modern commercial fast food is highly processed and prepared on a large scale from bulk ingredients using standardized cooking and production methods and equipment. It is usually rapidly served in cartons or bags or in a plastic wrapping, in a fashion which reduces operating costs by allowing rapid product identification and counting, promoting longer holding time, avoiding transfer of bacteria, and facilitating order fulfillment. In most fast food operations, menu items are generally made from processed ingredients prepared at a central supply facilities and then shipped to individual outlets where they are cooked (usually by grill, microwave, or deep-frying) or assembled in a short amount of time either in anticipation of upcoming orders (i.e., "to stock") or in response to actual orders (i.e., "to order").

Following standard operating procedures, pre-cooked products are monitored for freshness and disposed of if holding times become excessive. This process ensures a consistent level of product quality, and is key to delivering the order quickly to the customer and avoiding labor and equipment costs in the individual stores.

Because of commercial emphasis on taste, speed, product safety, uniformity, and low cost, fast food products are made with ingredients formulated to achieve an identifiable flavor, aroma, texture, and "mouth feel" and to preserve freshness and control handling costs during preparation and order fulfillment. This requires a high degree of food engineering. The use of additives, including salt, sugar, flavorings and preservatives, and processing techniques may limit the nutritional value of the final product.

Value Meals

A value meal is a group of menu items offered together at a lower price than they would cost individually. They are common at fast food restaurants. Value meals are a common merchandising tactic to facilitate bundling, up-selling, and price discrimination. Most of the time they can be upgraded to a larger size of fries and drink for a small fee. The perceived creation of a "discount" on individual menu items in exchange for the purchase of a "meal" is also consistent with the loyalty marketing school of thought.

Technology

In order to make speedy service possible and to ensure accuracy and security, many fast food restaurants have incorporated hospitality point of sale systems. This makes it possible for kitchen crew people to view orders placed at the front counter or drive through in real time. Wireless systems allow orders placed at drive through speakers to be taken by cashiers and cooks.

Drive through and walk through configurations will allow orders to be taken at one register and paid at another. Modern point of sale systems can operate on computer networks using a variety of software programs. Sales records can be generated and remote access to computer reports can be given to corporate offices, managers, troubleshooters, and other authorized personnel.

Food service chains partner with food equipment manufacturers to design highly specialized restaurant equipment, often incorporating heat sensors, timers, and other electronic controls into the design. Collaborative design techniques, such as rapid visualization and parametric modeling of restaurant kitchens are now being used to establish equipment specifications that are consistent with restaurant operating and merchandising requirements.

Consumer Spending

In the United States alone, consumers spent about $110 billion on fast food in 2000 (which increased from $6 billion in 1970). The National Restaurant Association forecasts that fast food restaurants in the U.S. will reach $142 billion in sales in 2006, a 5% increase over 2005. In comparison, the full-service restaurant segment of the food industry is expected to generate $173 billion in sales. Fast food has been losing market share to so-called fast casual restaurants, which offer more robust and expensive cuisines.

MAJOR INTERNATIONAL BRANDS

McDonald's, a noted fast food supplier, opened its first franchised restaurant in the US in 1955 (1974 in the UK). It has become a phenomenally successful enterprise in terms of financial growth, brand-name recognition, and worldwide expansion. Ray Kroc, who bought the franchising license from the McDonald brothers, pioneered many concepts which emphasized standardization. He introduced uniform products, identical in all respects at each outlet, to increase sales. At the same time, Kroc also insisted on cutting food costs as much as possible, eventually using the McDonald's Corporation's size to force suppliers to conform to this ethos.

Other prominent international fast food companies include Burger King, the number two hamburger chain in the world, known for promoting its customized menu offerings (Have it Your Way).

Multinational corporations typically modify their menus to cater to local tastes and most overseas outlets are owned by native franchisees. McDonald's in India, for example, uses lamb rather than beef in its burgers because Hinduism traditionally forbids eating beef. In Israel some McDonald's restaurants are kosher and respect the Jewish Shabbat; there is also a kosher McDonald's in Argentina. In Egypt, Morocco, Saudi Arabia, Malaysia, and Singapore, all menu items are halal.

North America

Many fast food operations have more local and regional roots, such as White Castle in the Midwest United States, along with Hardee's (owned by CKE Restaurants, which also owns Carl's Jr., whose locations are primarily on the United States West Coast); Krystal, Bojangles' Famous Chicken 'n Biscuits, Cook Out, and Zaxby's restaurants in the American Southeast; Raising Cane's in Louisiana; Hot 'n Now in Michigan and Wisconsin; In-N-Out Burger (in California, Arizona, Nevada, and Utah), Happi House in Northern California, and Original Tommy's chains in Southern California; Dick's Drive-In in Seattle, Washington and Arctic Circle in Utah and other western states; Halo Burger around Flint, Michigan and Burgerville in the Portland, Oregon area.

Also, Whataburger is a popular burger chain in the South and Mexico, and Jack in the Box is located in the West and South. Canada pizza chains Topper's Pizza and Pizza Pizza are primarily located in Ontario. Coffee chain Country Style operates only in Ontario, and competes with the famous coffee and donut chain Tim Hortons. Maid-Rite restaurant is one of the oldest chain fast food restaurants in the United States. Founded in 1926, their specialty is a loose meat hamburger. Maid-Rites can be found in the midwest - mainly Iowa, Minnesota, Illinois, and Missouri.

International brands dominant in North American include Wendy's, the number three burger chain in the USA; Dunkin' Donuts, a New England based chain; automobile oriented Sonic Drive-In's from Oklahoma City; Starbucks, Seattle-born coffee-based fast food beverage corporation; KFC, a part of the largest restaurant conglomerate in the world, Yum! Brands; and Domino's Pizza, a pizza chain known for popularizing home delivery of fast food.

Subway restaurants are known for their sub sandwiches and Subway is the largest restaurant chain to serve such food items. Subway has the second most stores of any chain restaurant system in the world after McDonald's, and the most locations in North America of any chain. Quiznos, a Denver based sub shop is another fast growing sub chain, yet with over 6,000 locations it is still far behind Subway's 34,000 locations. Other smaller sub shops include Blimpie, Mr. Goodcents, and Firehouse.

A&W Restaurants was originally a United States and North American fast food brand, but is currently an International fast food corporation in several countries.

In Canada the majority of fast food chains are American owned, or were originally American owned but have since set up a Canadian management/headquarters location in cities such as Toronto and Vancouver. Although the case is usually American fast food chains expanding into Canada, Canadian chains such as Tim Hortons have expanded into 22 states in the United States, but are more prominent in border states such as New York and Michigan.

Tim Hortons has started to expand to other countries outside of North America. The Canadian Extreme Pita franchise sells low fat and salt pita sandwiches with stores in the larger Canadian cities. Other Canadian fast food chains such as Manchu Wok serve North American style Asian foods; this company is located mainly in Canada and the USA, with other outlets on US military bases on other continents. Harvey's is a Canadian burger restaurant chain.

THE UNITED KINGDOM

In the United Kingdom, many home based fast food operations were closed in the 1970s and 1980s after McDonald's became the number one outlet in the market

. However, brands like Wimpy still remain, although the majority of branches became Burger King in 1989.

Japan

Traditional ramen and sushi restaurants still dominate fast food culture in Japan, although American outlets like Pizza Hut, McDonald's, and KFC are also popular, along with Japanese chains like MOS Burger.

Nigeria

In Nigeria, Mr. Bigg's, Chicken Republic, Tantalizers, and Tastee Fried Chicken are the predominant fast food chains. KFC and Pizza Hut have recently entered the country.

South Africa

KFC is the most popular fast food chain in South Africa according to a 2010 Sunday Times survey. Chicken Licken, Wimpy and Ocean Basket along with Nando's and Steers are examples of homegrown franchises that are highly popular within the country. Mcdonalds, Subway and Pizza Hut have a significant presence within South Africa.

China and Hong Kong

In Hong Kong, although McDonald's and KFC are quite popular, there are 3 major local fast food chains providing Hong Kong Chinese style fast food. These 3 major chains are Café de Coral, Fairwood Fast Food, and Maxim MX. In recent years, they have also been extending their operations to Mainland China.

Israel

In Israel, local burger chain Burger Ranch is popular as are McDonald's, Burger King and KFC. Domino's Pizza is also a popular fast food restaurant. Chains like McDonalds offer kosher branches. Non-kosher foods such as cheeseburgers are rare in Israeli fast food chains, even in non-kosher branches. There are many small local fast food chains that serve pizza, burgers and local foods such as falafel.

New Zealand

In New Zealand, the fast food market began in the 1970s with KFC (opened 1971), Pizza Hut (1974), and McDonald's (1976), and all three remain popular today. Burger King and Domino's entered the market later in the 1990s. Australian pizza chains Eagle Boys and Pizza Haven also entered the market in the 1990s, but their New Zealand operations were later sold to Pizza Hut and Domino's.

Two fast food chains were founded in New Zealand: Georgie Pie and Hell Pizza. Georgie Pie opened in 1977, and was based around the Australian and New Zealand meat pie. They went through a failed expansion attempt in the mid-1990s and became uneconomically viable, resulting in the chain being sold to McDonald's in 1996; the last Georgie Pie restaurant was closed in 1998. Hell Pizza was founded in 1996 in Wellington, and is known for its satanic marketing. Today, it has 64 stores in New Zealand, and also has stores in the UK, Australia, Ireland and Canada.

TRENDS

Health Concerns

Some of the large fast food chains are beginning to incorporate healthier alternatives in their menu, e.g., white meat, snack wraps, salads, and fresh fruit. However, some people see these moves as a tokenistic and commercial measure, rather than an appropriate reaction to ethical concerns about the world ecology and people's health. McDonald's announced that in March 2006, the chain would include nutritional information on the packaging of all of its products.

Consumer Appeal

Fast food outlets have become popular with consumers for several reasons. One is that through economies of scale in purchasing and producing food, these companies can deliver food to consumers at a very low cost. In addition, although some people dislike fast food for its predictability, it can be reassuring to a hungry person in a hurry or far from home.

In the post-World War II period in the United States, fast food chains like McDonald's rapidly gained a reputation for their cleanliness, fast service, and a child-friendly atmosphere where families on the road could grab a quick meal, or seek a break from the routine of home cooking. Prior to the rise of the fast food chain restaurant, people generally had a choice between greasy spoon diners where the quality of the food was often questionable and service lacking, or high-end restaurants that were expensive and impractical for families with children. The modern, stream-lined convenience of the fast food restaurant provided a new alternative and appealed to Americans' instinct for ideas and products associated with progress, technology, and innovation.

Fast food restaurants rapidly became the eatery "everyone could agree on", with many featuring child-size menu combos, play areas, and whimsical branding campaigns, like the iconic Ronald McDonald, designed to appeal to younger customers. Parents could have a few minutes of peace while children played or amused themselves with the toys included in their Happy Meal. There is a long history of fast food advertising campaigns, many of which are directed at children.

In other parts of the world, American and American-style fast food outlets have been popular for their quality, customer service, and novelty, even though they are often the targets of popular anger towards American foreign policy or globalization more generally. Many consumers nonetheless see them as symbols of the wealth, progress, and well-ordered openness of Western society and therefore become trendy attractions in many cities around the world, particularly among younger people with more varied tastes.

The fast food industry is a popular target for critics, from anti-globalization activists like José Bové to vegetarian activist groups such as PETA. In his best-selling 2001 book Fast Food Nation, investigative journalist Eric Schlosser leveled a broad, socioeconomic critique against the fast food industry, documenting how fast food rose from small, family-run businesses (like the McDonald brothers' burger joint) into large, multinational corporate juggernauts whose economies of scale radically transformed agriculture, meat processing, and labor markets in the late twentieth century.

While the innovations of the fast food industry gave Americans more and cheaper dining options, it has come at the price of destroying the environment, economy, and small-town communities of rural America while shielding consumers from the real costs of their convenient meal, both in terms of health and the broader impact of large-scale food production and processing on workers, animals, and land.

The fast food industry is popular in the United States, the source of most of its innovation, and many major international chains are based there. Seen as symbols of U.S. dominance and perceived cultural imperialism, American fast food franchises have often been the target of Anti-globalization protests and demonstrations against the U.S. government. In 2005, for example, rioters in Karachi, Pakistan, who were initially angered because of the bombing of a Shiite mosque, destroyed a KFC restaurant.

Practice of Dining

The practice of dining in is thought to have formally begun in 16th-century England, in monasteries and universities; though some records indicate that militaries have held formal dinners as far back as the Roman Legions. The Vikings held formal ceremonies to honor and celebrate battles and heroes. During the 18th century, the British Army incorporated the practice of formal dining into their regimental mess system.

Customs and rules of the mess were soon instituti-onalized rules, known as the "Queen's Regulations". The mess night or "Dining in" became a tradition in all British regiments. The Americans, taking many of their traditions from the British military, held mess nights in the 18th and 19th century, but the tradition waned after the Civil War.

During World War II, the custom was revived in the U.S. military, initially in the US Army Air Forces 8th Air Force, which was based in Britain. AAF Officers were invited to participate in host British military Mess Nights and then were obligated to reciprocate. Dining in took a temporary halt in the Navy and Marine Corps when Navy Secretary Josephus Daniels imposed prohibition of alcoholic drink, but soon the tradition was restored.

BRITISH ARMY TRADITIONS

By the early 19th century, the British Army's "mess night" developed formal rules, as a result of troops being stationed in remote areas. Officers elected mess committees to conduct their meals. The officers were expected to adhere to the rigid etiquette of Victorian-era society.

U.S. Traditions

Portions of the event tend to become quite humorous in nature, while others remain somber. Etiquette requires a diner to know what is appropriate at any given time.

The dining in follows established protocols. After a brief cocktail period of 30 to 45 minutes, the presiding officer, known as the "President of the Mess", announces, "Please be seated." The group will then retire to the dining area to be seated.

After tasting the meat (usually beef), the President will declare it "tasty and fit for human consumption", after which the meal will be served to the diners. After the dessert is finished, the President will invite the chief steward to bring forth wine and/or punch to be served, and toasting will begin. After the toasts have concluded, the floor will be opened to the levying of fines. The president and the guest of honor will have the opportunity to speak if they so desire. After this, the mess is often then returned to an open cocktail hour, and then the evening concludes with final honors.

The final and most solemn toast is always to fallen comrades. Often this tribute is marked with a display, including an empty table with a black tablecloth, inverted glass, blank dog tags, and a symbol representing tears (salt or lemon).

Some unusual forms of toasting are common to the U.S. and Canadian traditions. In the Toronto Scottish Regiment, for example, a loyal toast to the regiment's colonel-in-chief is performed standing with one foot on the chair and one foot on the dining table, facing a portrait of the C-in-C and drinking after the piper has played. Others, particularly Scottish regiments , perform toasts in the same way with one foot on a chair and one on the table. This is a frequent form of toasting in the United States Marine Corps as well. In the Scottish form, the glass is raised, lowered, brought out, and brought in, as the words of the toast, usually including some form of "Up", "Down", "To you", "To me", are recited, and finally drunk to the cry "Drink it up!" or similar.

Violations of Etiquette and Other Traditions

Violations of the formal etiquette of the dining in are "punished", generally with fines. The following are considered "Violations of the Mess":

- Untimely arrival at proceedings
- Smoking at the table before the lighting of the smoking lamp
- Haggling over date of rank
- Improper wear of uniform
  - o Inverted cummerbund (Note that U.S. Army regulation requires that cummerbunds be worn upside down: i.e. pleats down.)
  - o Wearing a clip-on bow tie at an obvious list
- Gaffes
  - o Loud and obtrusive remarks in a foreign language
  - o Foul language
  - o Discussion on a controversial topic (politics, religion, and women are commonly forbidden topics)
- Improper toasting procedure
  - o Toasting with an uncharged (empty) glass
  - o Rising to applaud particularly witty, succinct, sarcastic, or relevant toasts, unless following the example of the President
- Leaving the dining room without permission from the President of the Mess
- Carrying cocktails into the dining area before the conclusion of dinner
- Haggling over penalties or fines imposed
- Drawing a sword except in ceremony

At some mess nights, violators of the mess are obliged to publicly drink from a grog bowl in front of the mess attendees. The grog is sometimes contained in a toilet bowl, consisting of various alcoholic beverages mixed together. As a more disgusting effect, the grog may also contain floating solids, such as meatballs, raw oysters, or Tootsie Rolls.

The tradition of drinking grog originated with the British Navy. Grog consisted of the regulation rum ration diluted with water to discourage binge drinking. In modern times, grog comes in two varieties: alcoholic and non-alcoholic, the latter of which may contain anything that will make it less appealing to the taste, including hot sauce. For additional effect, the drinker may be required to drink from a boot.

In addition to visiting the grog bowl and paying fines, violators may be sentenced to sing songs, tell jokes, do pushups, or perform menial tasks to entertain the mess. In most cases, when a violator has been identified, he or she is given the opportunity to provide a rebuttal or defense for the violation, which rarely results in the violator being excused for the offense, and usually only results in more punishment.

Traditionally, all fines collected throughout the night are split amongst the stewards that served the attendees as a token of appreciation for their efforts. The fines can also be used to pay for the drinks consumed, while some units have used the Mess Night as a fund raiser (often to pay for a ball).

Members of the mess may also be singled out for some good-natured ribbing and teasing. In some units, members go out of their way to be picked on, often wearing obvious uniform violations, such as crowns, tiaras, eye-patches, bowties and cummerbunds of the wrong color, and other items that have no place on any military uniform. Some will attempt to leave sabotaging evidence on or around others they wish to see fined, so care must be taken to not be the butt of a joke.

Navy and Marine traditions also include that no diner may leave the hall to use the restroom without permission until Mr. Vice suggests that the company "shed a tear for Lord Admiral Nelson", a reference to the fact that his body was preserved in a barrel of brandy after his death at Trafalgar.

Most Messes attempt to furnish the night with military music and marches, with live bands if possible, or recorded music. Depending on how formal the ceremony is, the diners may be required to march to their seats.

In recent times, Marines have established a variant of the mess in a "field environment", subsituting in mess dress for utilities and combat equipment (to include camouflage facepaint), canteen cups, and tentage, while still retaining the formal nature of the ceremony.

Mess

. The root of mess is the Old French mes, "portion of food", drawn from the Latin verb mittere, meaning "to send" and "to put", the original sense being "a course of a meal put on the table". This sense of mess, which appeared in English in the 13th century, was often used for cooked or liquid dishes in particular, as in the "mess of pottage" (porridge or soup) for which Esau in Genesis traded his birthright. By the 15th century, a group of people who ate together was also called a mess, and it is this sense that persists in the "mess halls" of the modern military.

A mess is the place where military personnel socialise, eat, and (in some cases) live. In some societies this military usage has extended to other disciplined services eateries such as civilian fire fighting and police forces.

Canada

Messing in the Canadian Forces generally follows the British model, from whom most traditions have descended.

Basic regulations regarding the establishment and administration of messes is contained in the Queen's Regulations and Orders and the Canadian Forces Administrative Orders .

As in the British Forces, there are normally three messes: the Officers' Mess (called the Wardroom in Naval establishments), for commissioned officers and officer cadets; the Warrant Officers' and Sergeants' Mess (Navy: Chiefs' and Petty Officers' Mess), for senior non-commissioned officers and warrant officers; and the Junior Ranks Mess, for junior non-commissioned officers, privates, and seamen.

Some bases, such as CFB Kingston in the 1980s, had a Master Corporals' Mess separate from the Junior Ranks'; all of these, with the exception of the CFB Valcartier Master Corporals mess (known as the "Mess des chefs"), have since been amalgamated with the Junior Ranks' Messes.

Most bases and stations have three messes (Officers', Warrant Officers' and Sergeants', and Junior Ranks'). Many of these establishments have lodger units (such as Air Squadrons, Army Regiments, etc) who also have their own messes. All of Her Majesty's Canadian Ships have three messes aboard; this extends to Naval Reserve Divisions and other Naval shore establishments which bear the title HMCS.

Due to limited budgets and declining revenues, many messes have been forced to close or amalgamate: for example, at CFS St. John's, the Junior Ranks' Mess of Newfoundland Militia District closed, its members moving to the Station's Junior Ranks'; the Station's Officers' Mess and Warrant Officers' and Sergeants' Mess later amalgamated.

Headgear is not worn in Canadian Messes, except:

- by personnel on duty, such as a Duty or Watch Officer, or the Military Police;

- as permitted on special occasions, such as during costume parties, theme events, etc;
- by personnel for whom wearing headgear is mandatory (e.g. for religious reasons)

The usual "penalty" (which may only be executed if the offender voluntarily submits) applied to personnel who neglect to remove their headdress is to buy a round of drinks for the members present. The area from the entrance to the cloakroom, however, is normally considered a "neutral zone", and exempt from the no-headgear policy.

This prohibition is also extended to civilians, who are normally requested to remove their headdress upon entering; should they decline, they may be refused entry; they are not, however, normally subject to the "round for the house" rule.

All Canadian Forces personnel, Regular and Reserve, must belong to a mess, and are termed ordinary members of their particular mess. Although normally on Federal property, messes have been ordered to comply with the legal drinking age laws of their province; for example, an 18-year-old soldier may legally consume alcohol in a Quebec mess, but not in one in Ontario, where the legal age is 19. However, despite being underage, the soldier may not be prohibited entry into the mess.

Canadian Forces personnel are normally welcome in any mess of their appropriate rank group, regardless of element; thus a Regimental Sergeant-Major of an Infantry battalion is welcome in a Chiefs' and Petty Officers' Mess (inter-service rivalries notwithstanding). Personnel of a different rank (except as noted below) must ask for permission to enter; that may be granted by the President of the Mess Committee, his designate, or the senior member present.

The Commanding Officer of the establishment or unit that owns the mess is permitted access to all his messes; thus a ship's captain has access to his vessel's Chiefs' and Petty Officers' Mess, the Commanding Officer of a regiment may enter any of his regimental messes, and the Base Commander of a Canadian Forces Base is welcome in any of his base's messes. In practice, Commanding Officers rarely enter anything other than the Officers' Mess unless invited, as a point of etiquette.

In addition, duty personnel - such as a Duty NCO or Officer of the Watch - or the Military Police have access to any and all messes for the purposes of maintaining good order and discipline. Chaplains are usually welcomed in all messes.

As in the UK, Canadian messes are run by the Mess Committee, a group democratically elected by the members of the mess. One exception is on warships, where the president of the junior ranks mess is appointed by the Commanding Officer. The Committee members are generally the same as those of their British counterparts, with the addition of special representatives for such things as sports, housing, morale, etc. These positions are normally spelled out in the mess constitution.

Every mess has a constitution, which sets out the bylaws, regulations, and guidelines for such things as conduct of mess meetings, associate memberships, dress regulations within the mess, or booking of the mess by civilian organizations. The constitution and any amendments are voted upon by the members of the mess.

Germany

The Federal German Armed Forces (Bundeswehr) differentiates between three different mess areas.

1. HBG (Heimbetriebsgesellschaft) - More commonly called Enlisted Mess (Mannschaftsheim), it is

common for most bases to have one, where food and drink can be purchased, as well as newspapers and in some cases equipment and souvenirs (such as key chains etc,). There is generally no strict regulation of conduct, even though access is not limited to enlisted personnel, and NCOs or Officers may also be present, ensuring a more regulated conduct.

2. UHG (Noncommissioned Officers' Mess/ Unteroffizierheimgesellschaft(Gesellschaft lit. Society)) - Also called UK (NCO Comradeship/ Unteroffizierkameradschaft), this is the area where NCO can dine or spend their evenings. As opposed to the HBG, the UHG has a constitution, bylaws and a board. Access is usually restricted to NCOs, while Officers can gain entry, even though it is usually frowned upon by the NCO. Some Bases have a joint NCO and Officer's Mess.-

3. OHG (Officers' Mess/Offizierheimgesellschaft) - Also called Casino (Kasino or Offizierkasino). Much like the UHG, the Kasino also has a constitution, bylaws and a board. Gentlemanly conduct is mandatory. For instance upon entering the main hall, Officers are expected to stand at attention and perform a small bow. Additionally veteran's meeting are usually held either in a UHG or in a Kasino. As with the UHG, Kasinos have permanent personnel, as a general rule enlisted men, called Ordonnanzen(Military term for waiter or barman). Some 'Kasinos' have grand pianos, and hold recitals, as well as having music played during luncheons or dinners. Usually, official events, such also balls, but also unofficial events such as weddings, informational events and the like are held here.

The German Navy call their messes 'Messe', with the distinction Offiziermesse. The Land based messes are also called Offiziermesse.

India

The Indian Army follows a system similar to the British. A typical regiment/unit would have three messes, one for the commissioned officers, one for the Junior Commissioned Officers (JCO) and one for the NCOs. Havildars/Daffadars (equivalent to Sergeants) are considered to be NCOs. The Air Force however has an SNCO (Sr. NCO) mess for Warrant Officers and Sergeants, while lower-ranking NCOs would be members of the NCO's mess.

In the officer's mess and the JCO's mess, there also is rank of Mess Havildar. A Mess Havildar is a senior NCO who manages and executes the day-to-day activities of the mess.

On Republic Day (January 26) the JCOs are formally invited for cocktails at the Officers mess. This is reciprocated on Independence Day (August 15) by the JCOs.

ISRAEL

Navy

In the Israeli Navy, although Hebrew speaking, dining rooms on the Missile Boats, Dolphin submarines, and the kitchen in the Patrol Boats are named Messes, Crew Mess and Officers' Mess. Also, every special meal brought by a crewmember, say celebrating a birthday or a rank promotion, is called Mess. Few of the sailors in the Israeli Navy actually know the origins of the word, offering alternative explanations, such as "Short for Messiba (party in Hebrew)".

The word is probably left over from the Royal Navy.

United Kingdom

On a Royal Navy establishment, British Army garrison or Royal Air Force station, there are usually three Messes: the Officers' Mess, for Commissioned Officers; the Chief Petty Officer's or Warrant Officers' and Sergeants' Mess, for Senior Non-Commissioned Officers (SNCOs) and Warrant Officers (WOs); and the Junior Rates' Mess (JRM), for Junior Ranks, including Junior Non-Commissioned Officers. Officers and SNCOs usually live (if they are unmarried and do not want to live off base), eat, and socialise in their Messes, whereas Junior Ranks usually just eat there, being accommodated in barrack blocks and socialising in the NAAFI bar. A Regiment may also establish a Corporals' Club or Mess, of variable role and make-up.

There are various customs associated with the Messes. Senior Officers who visit an Officers' Mess will leave their hats on the table in the foyer to give fair warning of their presence. Headdresses are removed upon entering a mess (service personnel without headdress are "out of uniform" and thus cannot salute). The typical tradition is that anyone wearing a form of headdress inside the mess (due to forgetfulness or inexperience) must buy a round of drinks.

All service personnel belong to a Mess, which is typically located near the unit's HQ. Most Messes have dues (monthly or yearly, depending upon the Mess), and are non-profit. This allows the Mess to have substantially lower prices than civilian bars and clubs. Soldiers, sailors or air personnel are welcome in any Mess for their rank or equivalent, should they be away from their home unit, as long as they are paying dues in at least one mess.

Any serviceperson of a different rank (excluding the unit's Commanding Officer, the Duty Officer, duty NCO and Military Police) must ask permission to enter the Mess. There is no disciplinary sanction for not allowing personnel of higher rank into a mess at all or in a timely manner. A person is often required to buy a round to be allowed entry into a mess.

The main exceptions are for the Duty Officer and Duty NCO, who are required to keep order in the Mess. For the Warrant Officers' and Sergeants' Mess the CO is the Commanding Officer of the Mess, while the RSM or ranking Enlisted person is known as the Presiding Member. In Commonwealth armies an ex-enlisted officer such as the Quartermaster acts as the CO's representative/inspecting/ supervising officer.

A Mess is run by the Mess Committee, a group democratically elected by the members of the Mess (except Wardrooms), but normally agreed by the CO or RSM.

1. President of the Mess Committee - Mr PMC (Officers' Mess) or Chairman of the Mess Committee (Sergeants'/Petty Officers' Mess)
2. Vice President of the Mess Committee (Mr Vice), who is responsible for toasts during Mess Dinners. He or she is rarely the deputy of the PMC (normally this is the Secretary) but instead the most junior person in the Mess.
3. Treasurer
4. Secretary (Sec), who is responsible for records and minutes, etc.
5. Wines Member, who is responsible for keeping the bar stocked.
6. House Member, who is responsible for furniture and infrastructure.
7. Entertainments (Ents) Member, for any special events or parties in the mess.

Some messes also have a Senior Living-In Member (SLIM) who represents the living-in members and supervises their conduct.

Despite it being a democracy, the Commanding Officer (CO) of the unit has right of veto over the mess, and any large changes or events must have his approval. The CO is always allowed into any Mess (because they are legally all his), but it is often considered an abuse of power, unbecoming conduct or disturbing the order for a CO to drink in a lower rank mess, except when invited on special occasions.

The Officers' Mess in a Royal Navy ship or base is called the Wardroom. Associated with the Wardoom is a Gunroom, the mess for Midshipmen and occasionally junior Sub-Lieutenants. The Captain of a vessel is not normally a member of the Wardroom, which is always run by the First Lieutenant or Executive Officer (XO), thereby known as the Mess President ("Mess Prez"). This post is part of the job of being a ship's XO. Other committee members are generally appointed (voluntarily or otherwise) by the XO.

Mess dress is the military term for the formal evening dress worn in the mess or at other formal occasions. It is also known as mess kit. Mess dress would be worn at occasions requiring white tie or black tie.

MEALS AND MESSES

In some messes the reduction in the numbers of people living in the mess has caused facilities to be reduced for economy, and meals may be taken in another rank's mess. For instance, officers may eat in the SNCO's mess.

In this case, the officers will observe normal courtesies and seek out the senior member of the WO & SNCO's mess who is present, chat briefly and in doing so ask permission to use the mess, and also buy a drink at the bar (often buying for the senior person's group) as a way of offering some extra payment for the use of the mess beyond the meal payment between messes. A visiting person will not normally stay in the mess after the meal unless specifically invited by a member, and a higher ranking person will not assume that this invitation automatically applies to future occasions.

United States

Army

In the United States Army, officers historically have had to purchase their own food using funds allocated to each officer. In the far-flung forts of the old west officers would organize their food service in two ways: a "Closed Mess" was when the few officers of a small fort would pool all of their food funds to provide all meals to members only, thus being "closed" to outsiders except as guests; in a larger post, the larger pool of officers could allow the officers to purchase meals on an individual meal basis (after payment of a small monthly dues amount). Such arrangements were called "Open Messes".

The mess now is called a dining facility (DFAC). The Officers' Club is an outgrowth comparable to the Officers' Open Mess, but also providing areas to allow officers to entertain guests. Mess also describes the formal affair of having a "dining in", held for military members and closed to the public, or a "dining out", a social event for military personnel and their families.

United States Air Force

Social clubs on United States Air Force installations were at one time called Open Messes, even though most were known in vernacular as Officers Clubs or NCO clubs. At one time each squadron had its club, but these disappeared after World War II and the club became a facility of a base rather than a unit. Most are now officially referred to as officer or enlisted clubs; the term "mess" has largely disappeared from the Air Force lexicon.

Though a few bases (usually major training bases) have separate Airmen's Clubs for junior enlisted and NCO Clubs for noncommissioned officers, this is no longer normally the case. Physically separate Officers' Clubs are still the norm; however, smaller Air Force installations may have one consolidated club with separate lounges. Membership is voluntary, though highly encouraged for senior NCOs and officers. Most NCO and Officers Clubs contain a sit-down restaurant in addition to social lounges, meeting/dining rooms, and bars.

Mess halls in the USAF, where unmarried junior enlisted residing in the dormitories are expected to eat, are officially referred to as "dining facilities," but are colloquially called "chow halls," although dining facility workers traditionally take offense at the term.

CHAPTER–4

VALUABLE DRAWINGS AND PAINTINGS

Hotel décor has a few typical characteristics· It's expensive, nerve wracking and often quite frustrating to get even the basics like flooring turned into a working proposition. The hotel, after all, attracts people as much on the basis of its appearance and décor as it does on the basis of online bookings and reputation. Décor is, in fact, a major selling point.

The fact is that most hoteliers start with an existing décor, ongoing business, and have to plan through and around the logistic obstacle course that these factors create. Renovations take up time, money and space, and the process has to be done efficiently. Even starting from scratch, it's a big job.

RENOVATION FROM THE GROUND UP

The simplest approach is usually the best, and always the most cost-effective. Décor is after all a "look".

A bit of lateral thinking can do wonders:

What doesn't need doing? : This question alone can save you a fortune in time as well as money. If you've got a good basic layout, you can remove that from the equation, to start with. Good architectural features, good structure, and good floor space are all pluses. They can be enhanced, rather than "renovated on principle". (They're also often a selling point for return customers, so the makeover effect can be kept focused on the things that need doing.

Planning and Design: Having removed the things that don't need doing from the renovation, you can now start work like all professional renovators- With a basic structural plan. This plan saves more time, because it creates the environment for the renovations.

Here you can also get some help from technology. New interior design software, based on CAD in most cases, allows you to develop an entire renovation design, even if it involves building. This is "visualization" technology, and it's becoming extremely popular among professional designers because it allows clients to literally see what's possible.

The technology allows experimentation, design from scratch, and most importantly, and also provides options. Like the CAD software for construction, you can literally assemble a look. This software can also do individual rooms, work with measurements, and provide a very effective range of solutions.

Renovation According to Your Tastes

The technology is also a huge boon for hoteliers, who can present a fully costed, visible and intelligible design concept to hotel owners rather than the old maze of paper-based information. Hoteliers will also appreciate the fact that because this software is intended for the interior design market, appearances are very highly developed, and presentations look excellent.

Some industrial suppliers also have their own software for visualization. The most useful of these is the carpet visualization software which allows customization of carpet design, provides specifications, and permits full visualization of designs in context with their settings.

There's one other thing to know about these software design options- They're a lot of fun to work with. They provide scope for real creativity, and create good sounding boards for décor ideas. However big your hotel, and however demanding the renovation job, your renovation *starts* with plenty of choices.

Seven rare oil paintings by Armenian-American artist and Genocide survivor Arman Tateos Manookian (1904-1931) were removed from the historic Hotel Hana in Hawaii earlier this year, where they had been kept for more than 60 years. Considered daringly modern when they were first shown, the paintings are said to be worth six figures

What is it about a hotel room that is so appealing when you first open the door and step inside? The "initial impact" a hotel room has upon its customers is one of the most vitally important factors in the hotel business. Hotel decorators realize the psychological importance of "first impressions." People know what standards to expect when they enter a room or suite of an established brand-name hotel. If a customer's expectations are met in a positive manner, the customer will be back. If a customer's expectations are not satisfactorily met, the hotel will lose business. People talk. It's a fact of life in any business.

Five-star establishments set the standards for "first impressions." Their success depends on providing their guests a very pleasurable, if not awestruck, first impression, stimulating patrons' senses by sheer opulence and beauty. Lavish décor and architecture resonate within each and every suite.

The modus operandi of hotel decorating is incredibly simple. You can incorporate the basic elements of their systems of creating five-star luxury in your own home with little, if any, cost at all. Luxurious living is not necessarily reserved exclusively for the wealthy.

1. Upon entering a five-star hotel room, the first thing you consciously notice is that the room is well balanced. If there is one bed, it is centered on one wall. If there are two beds, they are distanced appropriately apart on the same wall while the armoire, dresser and television are generally located on the opposite wall, directly opposite the beds, creating a balance within the main area of the room. A sitting area, usually consisting of a small table and two chairs, is likewise centered in front of the window area.
2. The next thing you will consciously note as you enter your hotel room, is that the area is clean. Spotless. The sinks, tub, bathroom tile and fixtures literally shine and you subconsciously ask yourself, "How do they do that?" One important fact to remember is that hotel rooms are sanitized virtually every day. By getting into a habit of wiping out your own tub or shower unit with a damp towel after each bath or shower every day, you, too, can achieve the same effect.
3. The secret to glistening fixtures depends largely on the cleaning products that are used and how often they are applied. As for the actual cleaning products employed, a housekeeper's cart contains relatively few actual cleaning supplies. A high-quality all-purpose spray cleaner, furniture polish, window cleaner and an effective carpet and upholstery stain remover are the basic essentials.

   It's only a guess, but it appears that one good all-purpose cleaner is used to do most of the work on the fixtures and tile floors, generally amounting to nothing more than spraying it on and wiping it off. If this is done consistently, day after day, a room can't help but be clean. Lower-priced hotels may use something as basic as "Janitor In A Drum." The higher-priced places may use a much costlier variation, perhaps something like, "Jean e'Tour en la drumme."

Hotel rooms are also "spring cleaned" every few weeks. Curtains are removed, cleaned and replaced, lampshades and picture frames are dusted, mattresses are flipped and carpets are cleaned on a regular basis.

4. Probably the biggest secret of all to the cleanliness factor of a hotel room is that vacuuming is the final step of the hotel housekeeping operation. A hotel housekeeper will begin vacuuming at the far end of the room and make her way to the door as she completes her project, leaving an illusion that the area she leaves behind has never before been trodden. A freshly vacuumed area provides a psychologically inviting feeling. This is equally true on the home front.
5. The next thing you will notice in your freshly appointed hotel room is that the draperies are always open and natural sunlight floods the area. Lighting is an important factor of any room and natural sunlight gleaming into a sparkling clean area makes the shining mirrors, glass and lighting fixtures glisten that much brighter. If your initial entrance to the room is after dark, the streetlights, lights of the surrounding city or the outdoor lighting of the hotel courtyard likewise leave an important impact on your first impression of the room.
6. You will also notice that hotel rooms are always devoid of clutter. There is no unnecessary debris

taking up the surface space on the dresser, table or bathroom vanity. Simple, yet elegant displays of fresh, white fluffy towels and washcloths add just the right touch to the dressing area.

7. Basic hotel decorating begins with a neutral color scheme because neutral colors have a natural appeal to most everyone. When they stray from neutral tones in private rooms, decorators are quick to realize, they are venturing into unknown personal preference areas that simply do not appeal to everyone. Neutral colors are psychologically relaxing, non-hostile, soothing and comforting.
8. The color of a hotel room is provided in the bedspreads and either matching or coordinating curtains, which are generally always in earth-tone colors. The pictures on the wall likewise carry the color-scheme of the earth tone colors of green, brown and yellow with perhaps a splash of orange for effect.
9. Hotel rooms all share another common element of having quality, commercial grade furnishings and carpet, quality room-darkening draperies and bedspreads and the finest linens. Hotel towels and washcloths are consistently white and clean and are never stained or frayed.

Buying quality products for your own home is often less costly in the long run because quality products are more durable and last much longer than sub-standard merchandise. For example, cheap towels often fray after their very first encounter with a washing machine. After 3-4 washings, they look tattered and unsightly. High quality towels often continue to look fluffy and new even after 40-50 washings. Buying one quality towel instead of two or three cheap towels actually costs less in the long run because you don't have to replace them nearly as often.

- Having a few exceptionally high quality items instead of lots of low-quality goods takes up less space and makes you feel luxurious. Quality products go on sale, too.

10. The outstanding characteristic that sets a five star hotel above the rest, is the freshly cut flower and greenery arrangement that adds the final decorative touch to the area. Without much cost, you can grow your own garden and add this special affect whenever you feel a need to truly indulge.

By using these simple techniques, you, too can experience five-star luxury in your own home. It's the little things that make a very big difference.

How to Sell Your Paintings and Drawings?

Selling paintings and drawings is important to artists who wish to turn their hobby into a career. If you're an artist, then you know that selling your paintings and drawings can be quite a task. Fortunately, there are many options available if you know where to look. Getting your art on the market does not have to feel like an impossible feat.

1. Gather 10 of your best drawings and paintings. Take digital photos of all of your work and create a portfolio. The portfolio should include examples of all the types of work you do (human sketches, landscapes, pastels, etc.). You should include prices for the pieces you are displaying in the photos. Place all of these materials into a folder. This is your physical artist portfolio. You can also create a digital artist portfolio on ArtQ's website. Post the link to your portfolio on your social networking profiles or your website.

2. Look for stores in your area that might carry your paintings and drawings. Local gift shops, hobby shops, restaurants and coffee shops may be interested in displaying your work on consignment. Never pay them to carry your items. They only receive a percentage of the profit if they sell a piece of your art. You could also consider renting a booth at a flea market.
3. Set up an appointment with the owner of an art gallery. Many artists are hesitant about taking their work to an art gallery, but galleries are constantly looking for new work. Bring your portfolio and ask the gallery if they would consider displaying your work for sale.
4. Rent a booth at a local art and crafts show. Booths are priced based on the number of people expected to attend as well as the amount of booth space available. Display and sell your art in the booth. Be sure to place specific prices on the art and expect to negotiate. If you do not wish to negotiate, put up a sign that says so.
5. Promote your paintings and drawings online. Create a website or a blog showcasing your work. If you are hosting your own blog or website, let your visitors know that the paintings and drawings are for sale and either list your prices or provide information for how they may contact you.

Are you are thinking about building a restaurant? Here's some information on the Design & Construction process to give you a head-start, and some important promotional ideas after your dream is built.

Construction Documents

Typical Drawings

Building Codes

Special Agencies
Finding Consultants
Food Service Consultants
Certified (or licensed) Interior Designers
Architects
Misc. Consultants
Equipment Suppliers and Dealers
Hiring a General Contractor
Hiring a Graphic Artist, Web Designer and Publicist

Construction Documents

If you're going to build or remodel a restaurant, your general contractor will need a set of scaled construction documents, often called "working drawings". These documents can be drawn on a CAD system or by hand and consist of space plans, elevations, schedules and details. These drawings are generally prepared by several design consultants and engineers, integrated into one set for submittal to your local building and health department. The list of design consultants and engineers needed to prepare these drawings follows.

Typical Drawings

Here is a list of typical drawings you'll need for your building contractor (not in order)

- Cover Sheet with site and project information
- Demolition Plan, if applicable
- Store Front Elevations, if applicable
- Partition/Construction Plan
- Floor Plan with FF&E (furniture, fixtures and equipment)
- Environmental Plans for Health Dept.

- Finish Plans and Schedules
- Kitchen Equipment Elevations
- Wall Elevations
- Exhaust and Make-up Air Plan
- Refrigeration and Curb Plans
- Plumbing and Electrical Rough-in Plans
- Detail Drawings for custom cabinetry and fixtures
- Furniture and Equipment Specifications
- Reflected Ceiling Plan
- Electrical and Telephone Plans
- Title 24, California Only
- Mechanical Plan / HVAC Plan
- Door, Window and Ceiling Details

Building Codes

All your plans, drawings and specifications should be in compliance with the building and health codes that are applicable to your location. If your project is in California, the governing building codes are Title 24, the Uniform Building Code (UBC), Uniform Mechanical Code (UMC); and Uniform Plumbing Code (UPC). California Health Code governing restaurants is the California Uniform Retail Food Facilities Law (CURFFL).

Your drawings, plans, equipment and finish specifications should be approved by the following regulatory agencies:

- County Health Department
- Dept. of Building and Safety
- Fire Marshall

Special Agencies

Depending on your type of restaurant, equipment and geographical location, you may need approvals from:

- An air quality board such as the So. Calif. Air Quality Management District (SCAQMD) in Southern California
- An architectural review board or city planning commission.

And please remember, whether you are building new or remodeling, your restaurant must comply with the "Americans with Disabilities Act." as overseen by the United States Department of Justice.

Finding Consultants

It's a good idea to engage the services of various design professionals and food service consultants to help design and build your restaurant. Their expertise and guidance can help you save a great deal of time and money while also providing an attractive and functional restaurant.

As you probably already know, the first rule to hiring anyone is getting referrals from past clients and ask those clients lots of questions! How much experience did the consultant have in planning their type of facility? Did the consultant save the client money? Did they perform in a professional manner? Were they ethical? Did they do the work on time and on budget? Were their design solutions appropriate to the project? Would they hire the consultant again?

FOOD SERVICE CONSULTANTS

These individuals concern themselves with the kitchen (often referred to as "back of the house"). They will space plan your kitchen and service areas, recommend the best equipment for your menu and budget and give full specifications for the equipment you'll need. They generally do not sell equipment, so you should be getting an impartial opinion.

A good food service consultant's plans and specs should give enough information to get your plans approved by the local health department, secure bids from equipment dealers and general contractors. It's best to seek individuals with experience and a good reputation. Some food service consultants may become members of the Food Service Consultants Society International (FCSI).

Certified (or licensed) Interior Designers

Certified (or licensed) Interior Designers can plan for any part of your restaurant (for nonstructural work) and can usually submit plans to local building departments for permits. Generally, they perform all the design work your customers see, (also known as "front of the house").

The areas covered are exterior, entry, dining rooms, bars, eating counters and public restrooms. In California, designers certified by the California Council for Interior Design Certification (CCIDC) are the only recognized interior design professionals in the state (as defined in California Business & Professions Code). Seek the services of a Certified or licensed interior designer that has prior restaurant design experience.

Architects

These professionals can plan for any part of your restaurants structural or seismic building elements, usually utilizing the services of a Structural Engineer, and submit plans to the Dept. of Building and Safety. Some architects also do interior design work. In California, check with the Board of Architectural Examiners (BAE) in Sacramento for license verification. Also, ask for references and portfolios for the restaurants they have successfully completed.

Misc. Consultants

In addition, you may need the services of

- Electrical Engineers
- Mechanical Engineers
- Lighting Consultants
- Acoustical Consultants
- Audio Consultants

All the above consultants will work together on your behalf to produce a complete set of bid plans to submit to a general contractor, purchasing agent or dealer (prior to construction) so you can get an idea of cost and time involved for the opening of your restaurant.

EQUIPMENT SUPPLIERS AND DEALERS

These individuals or firms sell just about everything needed for the restaurant kitchen -- from heavy equipment to tabletop goods. Some equipment dealers also offer design and construction (turnkey services). These are valuable services which cost the dealer time and money to produce. Good design and planning take a great deal of education, time and experience. Please beware of deals that sound too good to be true, such as "free design" with purchase of equipment. You may not get the quality of design and services you need, and may run the risk of paying too much for your kitchen equipment.

Hiring a General Contractor

Be sure you hire a licensed general contractor who has good references and has experience in building restaurants. A residential contractor or one who has built office buildings and has no restaurant experience could cost the restaurant owner in lost time, quality of workmanship and price overruns.

If your project is going to be in California, be sure to verify the G.C.'s current active license with the California Contractors State License Board. This Board has published a free booklet entitled "What You Should Know Before You Hire a Contractor". Please call (800) 321-2752.

When hiring a general contractor, also make sure the contractor provides you with certificates of insurance for Workman's Compensation and General Liability (photocopies should not be accepted. Ask the contractor to have their insurance agent send them directly to you).

Hiring Other Professionals

When hiring all professionals, be sure to see their portfolios of work; ask for references, discuss their credentials, and be clear on the scope of work you want them to provide you. The following three professionals work can give you lasting value in establishing your public image, distributing your message and promoting your business.

Graphic Artist - for your logo, menus, stationery and other miscellaneous printed promotional material.

Web Site Designer - Do You Really Need a Website?

Publicist–You've spent lots of time and money planning and executing your dream. Don't believe the myth, if you build it--they will come. (Well, maybe if you have a prime location and your name is Wolfgang.) Even if your investors are high profile celebrities or your chef does cartwheels in the creme brulee, customers have to be clued into this phenomenon.

A publicist will send press releases to newspaper and magazine editors, restaurant critics, radio personalities and related Web sites. She/he will begin the buzz and leave their mouths craving for more. Your customers are continually looking to taste the newest trends or bite into brisket like mama made. A good publicist knows there's more news than what's on the menu. Press releases related to design and construction are sent to related trade publications and overcoming business obstacles and financing are sent to business editors. Everyone is hungry now.

Chapter–5

Food Service Management

Food service managers oversee the day-to-day running of restaurants, bars and "other establishments that prepare and serve meals and beverages to customers" according to the U.S. Department of Labor (DOL). Food service managers handle "all of the administrative and human-resource functions of running the business, including recruiting new employees and monitoring employee performance and training." They also work to make sure that customers are happy with their dining experience.

DIETARY MANAGEMENT

Dietary Managers specialize in providing optimum nutritional care through food service management. They work in hospitals, long-term care, schools, correctional facilities, and other non-commercial food service settings. Dietary managers are certified by the Dietary Managers Association (DMA), a national not-for-profit association.

In order to become a dietary manager, applicants must have a composite of education and experience that will allow them to take the Certified Dietary Manager Exam. The education and experience, along with passing the certification exam, certify Dietary Managers.

Dietary Manager Training

Dietary Manager Training Programs allow applicants to gain the education and experience needed to sit for the certification exam. A Dietary Manager Training Program consists of a minimum of 120 hours of distance education or classroom hours and a minimum of 150 hours of field experience. A Registered Dietitian oversees the entire field experience process.

Training programs consist of the following curriculum:

- Nutrition and Medical Nutrition Therapy
- Management of Food service Operations
- Human Resource Management
- Sanitation and Food Safety.

Food Service Management Institute

The Food Service Management Institute is a federal program that provides instruction, research, and materials in support of better food service management practices by child nutrition providers receiving federal support (e.g., schools operating school meal programs). It is permanently authorized under Section 21 of the National School Lunch Act (P.L. 79-396, as amended), with an annual entitlement funding level of $3 million.

U.S. Food Service

U.S. Food service, based in Rosemont, Illinois, is the second largest broadline food service distributor in the United States, behind Sysco. The company distributes food and related products to over 250,000 customers, including restaurants, healthcare facilities, lodging establishments, cafeterias, schools and colleges. U.S. Food service markets and distributes more than 43,000 national, private label, and signature brand items and employs 25,000 food service professionals.

The history of U.S. Food service encompasses the story of how (and where) Americans purchase the food they eat. It reflects the development of an entire industry, shifting from small entrepreneurial wholesalers supplying retail grocery stores to large regional and national distributors offering a broad line of products to institutional clients.

Early History

Several of the entities that comprised what is now U.S. Food service started in the 19th century. Monarch Foods, for example, traced its roots to Reid-Murdoch Co., a Dubuque, Iowa, company founded in 1853 to provision wagon trains heading west. Reid-Murdoch was a major sponsor of the "The Teenie Weenies" comic strip.

John Sexton & Company began as a retail tea and coffee merchant in Chicago, IL in 1883. John Sexton soon discovered hotels and restaurants were his biggest customers. By 1887, Sexton closed his four Chicago retail locations to focus on his institutional customers. By 1891, Sexton began manufacturing private label pickles, salad dressings, preserves, and jellies as well as roasting coffee in downtown Chicago.

In addition, Sexton established a food testing laborartory to guarantee that his products had a uniform high level of quality. Sexton also developed an extensive national institutional sales force in all major metropolitan areas as well as a catalog mail order grocery business. All national orders were shipped via rail or parcel post from Sexton's Chicago warehouse. Chicago delivers were by Sexton horse & wagon fleet and after 1924 Sexton electric and diesel truck fleets. By 1930, Sexton dropped the catalog mail order business and concentrated on the institutional customers throughout the United States.

In 1933, Sexton opened a warehouse and truck fleet in Brooklyn, NY to support the New York Sexton salesforce. By 1949, John Sexton & Co. was operating branch warehouses and truck fleets in Atlanta, Chicago, Dallas, Detroit, Long Island City, Philadelphia and Pittsburgh to support the Sexton national salesforce. In 1962, John Sexton & Co. was listed as a public company on the Over the Counter Stock Market with $79 million in sales and $2 million in profits.

In 1968, John Sexton & Co. had $90 million in sales , which represented 5% of the total institutional food service industry. In 1968, Sexton warehouses and truck fleets were located in Atlanta, Boston, Chicago, Cincinnati, Dallas, Detroit, Los Angeles, New York, Orlando, Philadelphia, St. Louis and San Francisco with a regional salesforce covering the majority of the United States.

This gave Sexton a coast to coast distribution and sales network to service their 70,000 customers. In late 1968, John Sexton & Co. was purchased by Beatrice Foods for $37.5 million in Beatrice preferred shares and assumption of Sexton debt. Beatric operated Sexton as an independent division until 1983, when Beatrice sold Sexton to S.E. Rykoff & Co of Los Angeles, CA for $84.5 million.

L. H. Parke Company started in 1889 as a partnership of Louis H. Parke and William P. M. Irwin. The partnership took over the small provision-pushcart business of Samuel Irwin, a civil war vet. who had lost his arm in the Battle of Winchester, Virginia. Parke started as a seller of coffee, tea and spices. The company grew to be a major institutional wholesale seller of canned goods and had five locations (Philadelphia, Pittsburgh, Washington, DC, Albany, New York and Richmond, VA.) by the time it sold out to Consolidated Foods in 1962. Donald Irwin Jr., President of Parke became the first president of Monarch Institutional Foods at that time.

Los Angeles-based S.E. Rykoff & Co. was established in 1911, and the Mazo and Lerch families started their business in Northern Virginia in 1927. Most of these wholesalers tended to specialize, selling items to local grocery stores. In the early 1930s, distributors, including Mazo-Lerch Company, began offering frozen foods, primarily frozen French fries and orange juice.

Post World War II

Food service distributors served institutional clients that provided food away from home, unlike retail distributors, who sold to grocery stores. The first distinction between the two groups came about in 1951, with the formation of the Association of Institutional Distributors. With fighting going on in Korea, the federal government reinstituted price controls, including a 16 percent ceiling on food distributors' gross profits. About a dozen companies met in Chicago to respond to that action. Because it cost more to distribute to their institutional customers than to grocery stores, the distributors wanted to be considered separately from grocery wholesalers and to have their ceiling raised to at least 21 percent. They were successful in their lobbying efforts.

The federal government also helped open up food service markets. Five years earlier, in 1946, the U.S. Congress passed the National School Lunch Act. Suddenly, large numbers of schoolchildren were eating cooked meals away from home, and school cafeterias became the first institutional mass market. One of the few distributors to focus on schools was the Pearce-Young-Angel Company (PYA) in the Carolinas. That same year, Consolidated Foods Corp., the precursor of Sara Lee Corporation, acquired Monarch Foods.

By the late 1950s, most distributors had added frozen foods to their product lines. In 1958, Mazo-Lerch held the first food show and was one of the first distributors to offer both custom-cut meats and beverage dispenser programs. The diversification trend continued over the years, as food service distributors provided disposable items such as napkins and tablecloths, followed by china and glassware, then light and heavy equipment.

The 1960s

In 1965, Americans spent just 20 cents of every food dollar for food away from home. Total distributor sales that year were an estimated $9 billion, and the average institutional distributor had an annual volume of $1.5-$2 billion. Institutional Distributor, in its first survey of the food service distribution industry, found that the average order size of respondents was $80.40, and the average number of customers was 572. The survey also found that nearly half of the respondents sold to both grocery and institutional customers. In 1962, John Sexton & Company went public and its shares traded on the Over the Counter Stock Market (NASDAQ) with $79 million in sales and $2 million in profits.

The 1970s

The decade of the 1970s saw the move to broadline, multi-branch organizations. Consolidated Foods bought the old Pearce-Young-Angel distribution network in 1971 and merged it with its Monarch Foods subsidiary to form PYA/Monarch. Sysco was established in 1970 by combining five independent wholesale grocery companies. Sysco went public in 1970 with $115 million in annual sales and shares were traded on the NYSE Continental Coffee Company established in 1915 by the Cohn family (CFS Continental) went public in 1970.

S.E. Rykoff & Co. was generating $1.9 milion in profits with revenue of $75.9 million and went pulic in 1972. In 1973, Continental Coffee Company changed their name to CFS Continental, Inc. to reflect the growing importance of food service to their traditional coffee business. By the end of 1979, SYSCO of Houston, TX has sales of $895 million. CFS Continental of Chicago, IL had sales of $775 million. PYA/Monarch of Greenville, SC had sales of $614 million, John Sexton & Company of Chicago, IL had sales of $350 million. S.E. Rykoff & Co. of Los Angeles, CA was generating $320 million strictly on the west coast.

The 1980s

The distribution industry went through a difficult period during the early 1980s, with companies under pressure as a result of inflation and economic slowdown. However, people still needed to eat, and much of the pressure was from competition. Speakers at national conferences focused on customer service, productivity, and professional development. Computers were playing a greater role in the business, enabling a distributor to provide customers with information to help control inventory, determine menu costs, and analyze profitability. As distributors became more professional, restaurant chains such as Marriott and Howard Johnson folded or reduced their self-distribution activities and focused on their restaurant operations.

By 1982, institutional food service distribution was a $69 billion industry. The five companies considered "national distributors," were PYA/Monarch, John Sexton & Company,($360 million in sales) a division of Beatrice Foods, Sysco Corporation of Houston ($1 billion in sales), CFS Continental, Inc. ($1 billion in sales), and Kraft Food service. The five companies had a total of 168 distribution centers covering major portions of the country. Despite the geographical dominance, these five multi-branch distributors reported combined sales in 1982 of $4.8 billion - 7 percent of the industry.

Over the next several years, the big distributors made major acquisitions. S.E. Rykoff bought John Sexton & Company in 1983 for $84.5 million, in what was then the largest acquisition in the industry. The renamed Rykoff-

Sexton took fourth place among food service distributors with $800 million in sales. CFS Continental's purchase of Publix Fruit and Produce moved it into third place, with sales in the $1.1 billion range.

Number one Sysco acquired B.A. Railton along with Pegler, increasing its volume to over $2 billion. In Meanwhile, in Greenville, South Carolina, number two PYA/Monarch bought Fleming Food service of Austin, Texas, raising its 1984 sales volume to an estimated $1.3 billion. By the end of its fiscal year in June 1984, PYA/ Monarch was serving some 70,000 food service operators, and its 22 distribution centers blanketed 60 percent of the United States.

PYA/Monarch was one of the first distributors to compete as a provider of services as well as products. "The day of the distributor who merely warehouses, delivers, and takes orders for products a customer wants is over," company management told Institutional Distribution in a 1984 article. PYA/Monarch's mission statement revealed its goal: "... to be a premier company in every area of operations, providing products and services that can enable a customer to run a more efficient and profitable business."

Using the largest computer in the industry, PYA/ Monarch phased in a new state-of-the-art data processing system. Totally centralized, the system made it possible for headquarters to carry out data processing for each of the 22 branches, whose computers now gathered data.

The 1980s saw a tremendous change in the eating habits in the United States. By 1986, Americans were spending one-third of every food dollar outside the supermarket, and the food service distribution had grown to a $78 billion industry.

By April 1989, Sara Lee Corporation had decided to sell off the northern division of PYA/Monarch, citing dissatisfaction with its performance. Although the southeast division was the top food distributor in its region, overall PYA/Monarch ranked third behind Sysco and Kraft, and Sara Lee was committed to being first or second in each of its businesses.

In June 1989, members of PYA/Monarch management incorporated a new entity, JPF Holdings, Inc. Two weeks later, on July 3, JPF Holdings acquired all the capital stock of the Sara Lee subsidiary, JP Food service Distributors Inc, including the mid-Atlantic and northeastern operations of PYA/Monarch Inc. Under the terms of the leveraged buyout, Sara Lee retained ownership of PYA/Monarch, now operating in the southeast, as well as 47 percent of the shares in JP Food service.

Headed by James L. Miller, who had been executive vice-president of PYA/Monarch's northern division, the new company immediately sold three of its branches - Los Angeles, Little Rock, and Paducah - to Kraft Food service. The result was a major regional operation with nine distribution centers serving a territory from Virginia north to Maine and west to Nebraska.

JP Food service Distributors passed the $1 billion mark in its first year, with sales for fiscal 1990 of $1.02 billion. That was a jump of more than 12 percent from the division's sales in fiscal 1989, and made the new company number five among the top 50 distributors selected by Institutional Distributor. But Miller and the other managers had borrowed over 95 percent of the $317 million they paid for the company. With that amount of debt, and with a soft economy, JP concentrated on building the lowest cost structure in the industry. The company invested primarily in improving facilities, adding a new $15 million replacement center between Washington, D.C., and Baltimore and building an addition at its Allentown, Pennsylvania warehouse that doubled freezer and cooler capacity. It also used technology to cut costs and provide greater service to its customers. For example, a hand-held electronic device allowed JP customers to monitor their inventory and send information to the company.

The 1990s

In November 1994, five years after it was created, the company adopted the name JP Food service, Inc. and went public in November, listed on the NASDAQ under the symbol JPFS. Sara Lee Corporation now held 37 percent of JP common stock. The public offering raised $86 million, and JP restructured and paid off much of its debt.

JP Food service had more than 21,000 customers in 25 states in the Mid-Atlantic, Midwest, and Northeast regions of the country and was the sixth largest food distributor. It provided customers with a broad line of products, including canned, dry, frozen, and fresh foods, paper products, detergents, and light restaurant equipment. With its debt problems resolved, the company set a new growth strategy which, in addition to increasing internal growth, included acquiring smaller distributors. Its first purchases were Tri River Foods, Inc. and Rotelle Inc., two Pennsylvania distributors. JP's strategy also called for increasing its line of private label products, which included Hilltop Hearth breads, Cattlemen's Choice meats, and Roseli Italian foods.

Food service distribution had grown to become a $124 billion industry, and the ten largest distributors accounted for 18 percent of the business. JP's business, which for fiscal 1995 reached $1.12 billion, was about 55 percent independent (hospital cafeterias, family-owned restaurants) and 45 percent chains. The increasing product demands and bigger menus of the chains and large restaurants were important factors fueling consolidation among distributors.

Toward the end of 1995, the company and its former parent, Sara Lee Corporation, began talks about exchanging PYA/Monarch, Sara Lee's southeastern food service subsidiary, for JP stock worth about $946 million. Yet, the two companies failed to reach agreement on several factors, including valuation (JP's stock price had gone up in expectation of the merger), structure, and dilution of earnings to existing shareholders, and the deal fell through in February 1996. The experience left both sides bitter, and JP was expected to find a way to reduce Sara Lee's presence or end its investment in the company all together.

That separation occurred before the end of 1996, when JP held a public offering involving the sale of all the common stock held by Sara Lee. On December 31, 1996, JP Food service moved to the New York Stock Exchange, trading under the symbol JPF.

JP continued buying smaller companies, paying for them with $66 million raised by another stock offering. Acquisitions included Valley Industries of Las Vegas, Arrow Paper and Supply Company, based in Connecticut, Squeri Food Service of Cincinnati, and Mazo-Lerch Company, Inc., the 70-year-old food distributor based in northern Virginia that had held the first food fair in 1953.

By the end of the fiscal year in June, net sales were up 17 percent to $1.7 billion, with acquisitions accounting for about six percent of the increase and the remaining 11 percent from internal growth. JP's growth was significantly higher than the three percent for the food service distribution industry. The JP Food service company credited its internal growth to sales training and promotions and to the expansion of its private and signature brands.

U.S. Food Service

The name "US Food service" comes from United Signature Foods, Inc. , a broadline distributor based in

Wilkes-Barre, PA. US Food service Inc was formed in March 1992 by Unifax Inc specifically to acquire the White Swan Inc, a Dallas-based distributor. The merger with White Swan Inc was completed in October 1993. Via a share exchange (shares of White Swan were swapped for shares of US Food service), it created one of the largest broadline distributors in the country.

The resulting combined entity had five operating subsidiaries: White Swan, Bevaco Food Service, Kings Food service Inc., Roanoke Restaurant Service and Biggers Brothers Inc, thus operating food service distribution centers in Pennsylvania, North Carolina, Tennessee, Virginia, Texas, Ohio, West Virginia, Oklahoma and Florida. Merrill Lynch Capital Partners, a wholly owned subsidiary of Merrill Lynch & Co., owned a controlling ownership in both White Swan and US Food service, by virtue of its funding each company's leveraged buyouts - White Swan in 1988 and Unifax Inc in 1992. The US Food service management team will include Frank Bevevino, president and chief executive; Thomas G. McMullen and Peter Smith, vice presidents; David F. McAnally, vice president and chief financial officer; and William Griffin, vice president of administration.

In 1995, US Food service of Wilkes Barre, PA was the 4th largest broadline food service distributor, according to Institutional Distributor Magazine, behind Sysco (#1), S.E. Rykoff/John Sexton (d.b.a. Rykoff-Sexton) (#2), and Kraft Food service (#3), and just ahead of JP Food service (#5), and PYA/Monarch (#6).

Within the next 12-24 months, S.E. Rykoff/John Sexton would establish a solid hold of this #2 spot by acquiring Continental Foods of Baltimore, MD, H&O Foods of Las Vegas, NV, and US Food service. Rykoff-Sexton management created the Rykoff-Sexton Funding Corporation to finance the acquisition of their near competitor US Food service, and by the end of 1996 the newly renamed and much larger corporation was now trading on the New York Exchange as Rykoff-Sexton Inc.

US Food service had now become a division of Rykoff-Sexton Inc. The Rykoff-Sexton Inc. parent corporation was now operating a handful of divisions, a broadline food service distribution division (d.b.a. "US Food service" after combining with the S.E. Rykoff and John Sexton & Co distribution divisions), a private label manufacturing division (historical food service brands like John Sexton and SERCO), a food service contract and design division (historically known as Finegolds), and food service equipment and supply (2nd in size at the time to only Edward Don & Company).

Rykoff-Sexton Inc management was not done yet, negotiations were already underway in 1997 to combine with JP Food service. Mark Van Stekelenburg, then Chairman of the Board and Chief Executive Officer of Rykoff-Sexton Inc, and the former President and Chief Executive Officer of G.V.A., Inc, the largest food service distributor in the Netherlands and a subsidiary of Royal Ahold N.V., had led the 2nd largest food distributor Rykoff-Sexton Inc. into the combination of the industry's #2, #4, and #5 largest corporations in less than 24 months. In early 1997, Mark Van Stekelenburg said, "Rykoff-Sexton Inc./U.S. Food service will be the number 1, number 2, or number 3 player in every market in which it serves the broadline food service distribution business."

In late 1997, JP Food service ($1.7 billion in revenues) jumped into second place among food service distributors with the consummation of a merger with rival Rykoff-Sexton Inc (with just under $5 billion in revenues) for $1.4 billion. Unlike previous acquisitions that JP Food service had undertaken, the merger with Rykoff-Sexton was much bigger.

Sales were expected to triple, to $6 billion, and the number of JP Food service customers ballooned to 130,000. As a result, Standard & Poor's added JPF to the S&P MidCap 400 Index. The merger also changed JP Food service from a major distributor in the East and Midwest into one operating coast to coast. New territories included the Southeast, the Sun Belt, and the West Coast.

The Reemergence of U.S. Food Service

Mark Van Stekelenburg in early 1998, now a Director on the JP Food service Board, Vice Chairman of the JP Food service Board, and President of JP Food service, gave the reins of the corporation to Jim Miller, and returned to Royal Ahold N.V., (NYSE: AHO [ADR]), the leading international food provider with major operations in the US, Europe and Latin America. Shortly after the departure of Mark Van Stekelenburg, JP Food service changed its name to U.S. Food service. Thus the reemergence of the U.S. Food service corporation, previously privately held in 1995, as of Monday, March 2, 1998, the trading symbol was changed from "JPF" to "UFS" and was now being traded publicly on the New York Stock Exchange.

Acquisitions continued even as the new U.S. Food service (NYSE: UFS) worked to assimilate the Rykoff-Sexton operations, adding Sorrento Food Service, Inc., of Buffalo, Westlund, a Minnesota custom cut meat specialist and a number of other smaller food service companies.

By mid-1998, Chairman and CEO Jim Miller was proud of the accomplishments, telling the Baltimore Sun, "We not only successfully completed the largest merger ever in our industry, tripling the size of our company, we did so achieving record earnings and meeting or exceeding virtually every goal set out in our merger plan." In the 3rd quarter of the calendar year 1998, U.S. Food service announced it was selling the assets of its Rykoff-Sexton manufacturing division as part of its plan to shed its non-core operations.

The successful integration of the larger Rykoff-Sexton company made U.S. Food service a favorite among analysts, and the company itself indicated it was still on the lookout for purchases in the highly fragmented food service industry.

One year later, 1999, fiscal 2000, U.S. Food service is generating sales that exceed $7 billion and has caught the attention of Royal Ahold N.V. (NYSE: AHO [ADR]). Within the first quarter of calendar year 2000, Royal Ahold has filed a tender offer, filed by Ahold Acquisition, Inc. and Koninklijke Ahold N.V. with the U.S. Securities and Exchange Commission, to purchase all outstanding shares of U.S. Food service.

Post 2000

U.S. Food service becomes division of Royal Ahold NV March 20, 2000, U.S. Food service agreed to be acquired by Royal Ahold for $26 per share or $3.6 billion.

To strengthen its presence in the southeastern United States, U.S. Food service acquired former sister company PYA/Monarch for $1.57 billion on December 5, 2000. The acquisition meant U.S. Food service's sales would now reach $12 billion annually.

In November 2001, the U.S. Food service division of Ahold, acquired Alliant Exchange Inc., parent company of Alliant Food service. This greatly expanded the geographical range of its activities. In fact, U.S. Food service said Alliant would give it access to 21 new U.S. markets. This $2.2 billion purchase gives U.S. Food service distribution centers and food processing facilities in areas that are serving 100,000 customers-including independent and multiunit restaurant operations, hotels, contract food service operations and healthcare facilities.

In 2000, Alliant Food service reported revenues of $6.6 billion. (Kraft Food service became Alliant Food service in 1996 after Clayton, Dubilier & Rice, Inc. purchased the Kraft Food service division from the Philip Morris Corporation).

After the Alliant acquisition, U.S. Food service was now generating combined total revenues of approaching $14 billion. U.S. Food service growth was 600% over the last 6 years, from about $2 billion in revenues in 1995, to $14 billion in late 2001.

The making of U.S. Food service reflects the trends of its industry: from retail to institutional customers; from specific products to a broadline of offerings; from single distribution centers to multi-unit branches; increased professionalism and customer service; and, most pronounced, the continuing and aggressive expansion through acquisition.

U.S. Food service taken private by investment funds During 2006 there was much speculation as to which equity firm would acquire U.S. Food service from Royal Ahold. Ahold had refused to consider a spinoff of the subsidiary to the capital markets, and appeared to be headed toward an auction that JP Morgan would manage.

This was consistent with many larger going concerns in the United States that appeared to be headed away from being publicly traded in what many believed was an attempt to avoid the requirements of the Sarbanes-Oxley Act of 2002. After the internal accounting controls and procedures struggles that U.S. Food service had gone through over the past 3 years-the very same that the Sarbanes-Oxley Act of 2002 was designed to address-one had to wonder if U.S. Food service being privately held was the proper path toward a transparent valuation of the company.

On May 2, 2007, Clayton, Dubilier & Rice, Inc. (CD&R) and Kohlberg Kravis Roberts & Co. L.P. (KKR) announced a definitive agreement to acquire U.S. Food service from Royal Ahold. Funds affiliated with CD&R and KKR are equal partners in the transaction, valued at $7.1 billion.

The Washington Post quoted Robert S. Goldin, an executive vice president at Technomic, a food consulting firm in Chicago, as saying, "When Ahold acquired U.S. Food service, the industry consensus was that it overpaid." Industry analysts had previously estimated U.S. Food service could be worth $5.1 billion to $5.7 billion, the Post reported, adding that industry experts now agreed that Ahold got top dollar.

"For Ahold this is a reasonably good end to what's been a pretty unsuccessful foray into U.S. food distribution," Goldin continued. "It's been a sore spot for them. They overpaid for the business and never rationalized it. I would imagine they are pretty happy to put this one behind them."

The Post added that "Ahold was forced to restate more than $800 million in earnings after it came to light that U.S. Food service executives had inflated promotional rebates from suppliers to meet earnings targets. The scandal caused the parent company's shares to plunge."

"Ahold settled with the Securities and Exchange Commission two years ago and agreed to pay $1.1 billion to resolve shareholder lawsuits."

On August 13, 2010, U.S. Food service announced that John A. Lederer was appointed president and chief executive officer effective September 8, 2010.

SPECIALTY DIVISIONS AND COMPANIES

North Star Food Service

In May 2005 U.S. Food service announced its chain restaurant division will operate under the name North

Star Food service. North Star, which employs 2,100 associates in 11 locations throughout the U.S., serves high-profile regional and national chains. Support office is located in Greenville, South Carolina.

North Star Food service sales in 2005 were $2.8 billion, with the unit shipping more than 114 million cases of product to America's leading restaurant companies.

Next Day Gourmet

The company has a supply and equipment division Next Day Gourmet which offers direct order and online purchasing of S&E equipment. Next Day Gourmet provides restaurant startup equipment order fulfillemnt through the local distribution facility and sales representative.

Monarch Foods

To further boost sales growth in the broadline division, U.S. Food service will pare its portfolio of 60 private-label brands down to 20. A new unit within the broadline division, called Monarch Foods, will focus on these "power brands." Robert Aiken, currently working on marketing and supply chain efforts for U.S. Food service, will head Monarch Foods.

Alliant Logistics

US Food service is launching the formation of Alliant Logistics. This formation a "company within a company" is designed to allow US Food service to take full advantage of its logistics network, increase customer support and better leverage the organization's position in the market place. This model will incorporate the development of regional logistics centers in Rosemont, Illinois; Phoenix, Arizona and Ft. Mill, South Carolina.

Stock Yards

In February 2000, Stock Yards Packing was sold to U.S. Food service. U.S. Food service owned seven other custom meat cutters at the time and wanted to add a company with a solid reputation to its mix. Other pluses in acquiring Stock Yards were that company's strong management and labor force; their excellent customer service; reputation for high-quality products; and the fact that Stock Yards was a Certified Angus Beef distributor. Dan Pollack stated at the time of the acquisition that he hoped to use Stock Yards's expertise to streamline and standardize the meat cutting operations of U.S. Food service.

CHAPTER–6

FOOD SERVICE'S THEORY OF EVOLUTION

Harland Sanders was nearing desperate straits when in 1952 he visited Leon W. "Pete" Harman in an effort to persuade the Salt Lake City restaurateur to sell his specially seasoned chicken.

After 13 years of perfecting an herb-and-spice chicken recipe at his roadside restaurant, Sanders, a former streetcar conductor and justice of the peace, recently had learned that he was going to be a former operator as well. The new interstate 75 was planned to bypass his hometown of Corbin, Ky., taking with it much of the traffic that had patronized the long-popular Sanders Court & Cafe.

So Sanders, then 66 years old, hit the road, lugging his secret recipe, a pressure cooker and a lofty plan to make his fortune by allowing other restaurateurs to add his chicken to their menus in return for a few cents each time the product was sold. Harman, who knew a good deal when he tasted it, obliged. Together, the two pooled their talents and began to build the world's largest quick-service chicken chain.

"I was the first franchisee, so it was a handshake thing," recalls Harman, founder of 264-unit Harman

Management Corp. in Los Altos, Calif. "There were no other documents floating around."

In the 46 years since then the relationship between KFC Corp. and its franchisees has grown far more complex. As the chain took flight and the white-suited colonel became one of the country's most recognizable icons, several suitors came looking for their share of the proceeds. Along the way the rules of empire-building changed. and the simple franchise relationship vanished forever.

Investors Jack Massey and John Y. Brown bought the business during the 1960s, and Heublein stepped up to the plate in 1971. Each purchase tested the franchisor-franchisee bond, but it was after PepsiCo Inc. made its bid in 1986 -- six years after the beloved colonel's death -- that the relationship nearly hit the skids.

In 1989 Harman -- the man who coined the phrase "Kentucky Fried Chicken" and soon after had the evolutionary idea to put the chicken in a bucket with potatoes, biscuits and gravy and market it as a meal -- joined other franchisees in a bitter legal battle over a new franchise contract. The dispute raged on for seven years, crippling the trust that had helped the system thrive. The company, which now operates 9,000 outlets worldwide, still is working to recapture the fragile balance of franchisor and franchisee interests crucial to longevity.

"One thing we all recognized is that we couldn't settle without it being a win-win for both parties," David Novak, former head of KFC and current leader of KFC-parent Tricon Global Restaurants, said when the settlement was announced. "But our job really has just begun. There's more pressure on us now to work closer together."

KFC's growing pains are by no means unique or isolated. As franchise systems have matured and competition within the food service industry has increased, many a chain has found itself plagued by the dual challenges of continuing to grow a concept without choking the livelihoods of existing franchisees.

The widespread use of nontraditional locations only complicates the conundrum.

"The challenge today has less to do with franchising than it has to do with different segments of the industry," says Larry Hantman, senior vice president and general counsel for Randolph, Mass.-based Allied Domecq Retailing USA, which operates the Dunkin' Donuts, Baskin Robbins and Togo's chains.

"As the industry matures, the number of franchised units in any one segment increase and competition intensifies," Hantman explains. "So individual franchising systems have to keep concepts alive, keep them meeting consumer expectations and keep them vibrant.

"Franchising works best when it's growing," he continues. "It's a business, and the major challenge is not to get involved in the internecine battle on how you divide the pie, but how do you grow the pie? Is the product all it can be? The constant striving for excellence within the system -- that is the challenge."

SEWING UP A NEW KIND OF DEAL

Widely accepted as the fastest means by which to distribute a product, franchising has proved over the decades to be both savior and sore spot. While many people have struck it rich linking their destiny to a franchise system, many also have kissed their life savings goodbye. Just as surely, franchisors imbued with honest dreams of creating thriving and mutually beneficial enterprises have been undermined by crooks perpetuating scams that depleted the wallets and souls of unsuspecting victims.

Today franchising accounts for nearly 41 percent of all retail sales in the United States, or $800 billion annually, according to statistics published in 1996 by the Washington, D.C.-based International Franchise Association. The group estimates that there are about 550,000 franchised businesses in the United States alone, employing 8 million people. And, the IFA estimates, a new franchise opens every eight minutes.

"Franchising is growing very rapidly worldwide," says Mahmood Khan, Ph.D., head of the Department of Hospitality and Tourism Management at Virginia Tech in Blacksburg, Va. "It started first in the United States, and now almost 60 percent or more of the business in restaurants is franchising."

Although franchising has paid off hadsomely for untold numbers of chicken, hamburger, pizza and sandwich purveyors, food service operators were some-what slow to seize its benefits.

Stan Luxenberg, in his book "Roadside Empires: How the Chains Franchised America," credits sewing machine-manufacturer I.M. Singer & Co. with creating the country's first franchise system in the early 1850s. In reality, what the New York-based company created was a network of dealers. Singer established a plan whereby salesmen across the country paid a fee for the right to sell sewing machines in designated territories. Not only did the salesmen pay for their territory, but also they paid $60 for machines, which they would then sell for $125.

Singer's intent was to distribute its product more widely, and while the method proved successful in making the sewing machine a more common household appliance, it did not make Singer money. The structure of the system profited dealers more than the parent company. By 1856 Singer began repurchasing the rights to its territories.

"Though the Singer scheme failed, it did break new ground," Luxenberg wrote in his 1985 book. "In attempting to solve its distribution problems, the company had established a primitive franchise system, probably the first used by American business and the ancestor of the elaborate networks employed by today's hamburger and motel chains."

Car manufacturers were next to adopt the dealer method of distributing their goods in the late 1890s. Soon after gas station operators caught on. Meanwhile, food service operators would not capitalize on franchising for almost another 30 years.

Food Service Enters Franchising Fray

The first food service operator to embrace franchising was Howard Dearing Johnson, a debt-plagued former cigar salesman who stumbled on redemption when he took over a failing drugstore in Quincy, Mass., in 1925.

Upon acquiring the store, Johnson set about reviving its soda fountain sales by developing a rich chocolate syrup and upgrading the ice cream. Soon crowds were flocking for his proprietary butterfatladen 28 flavors.

But Johnson's fiscal woes did not immediately subside, and he found himself borrowing money to extend his menu line and to open new units. With a couple thousand dollars from one friend he hired a cook and added sandwiches, sirloins and booths to his operation. Another $500 loan allowed him to open a second ice-cream store on a beach in Wollaston, Mass., in 1927. In 1928 he opened a third store in Nantasket Beach, Mass.

The two beach stores each performed fabulously, pulling in $30,000 and $50,000, respectively, within months of their openings. Despite his success, however, Johnson -- known to have a lax attitude toward his creditors -- still had a hole in his pocket. Although he wanted to open more stores, his lingering debt and the gathering Depression scuttled his plans. Then Reginald Sprague entered the picture.

Sprague had offered to rent Johnson space for another summer ice-cream stand when Johnson instead suggested that the partnership could be more fruitful if Sprague ran the restaurant himself. For a fee Sprague received the right to use the Howard Johnson's name, product and operations blueprint. A franchise chain was born.

"In retrospect it is evident that the guy had a tremendous vision at a time when the industry was just getting its start," Thomas Russo, chairman, president and chief executive of Braintree, Mass.-based Ground Round Restaurants Inc. and a 20-year veteran of Howard Johnson's once commented to Nation's Restaurant News. Ground Round, a casual dinner-house concept, became in the 1970s the growth vehicle for the then-stagnating Howard Johnson's chain.

"He implemented single-sourcing and orange roofs and provided a quality product when there were no alternatives for finished or semifinished quality products," Russo explains. "In those days they just weren't there. At the same time he introduced a control factor and realized the consistency of a product was important if you were to have a large chain."

Johnson's ambition quickly outgrew Massachusetts. Aware that the automobile was making Americans increasingly mobile, in 1940 he secured the rights to develop on the Pennsylvania Turnpike. By the time of the company's initial public offering in 1960 about 650 Howard Johnson's -- by then sporting a trademark orange roof and weathervane -- resided strategically along the country's best-traveled East Coast roads.

Food service franchising "basically grew up along the highways, primarily because people wanted standardized meals," notes Tom Dicke, associate professor of history at Southwest Missouri State University in Springfield, Mo. "...Howard Johnson catered to people going to Florida.

They stopped because they knew what they were going to get and what they were going to pay for it."

The Race is On

Others soon followed in Johnson's franchising footsteps. Quincy, Mass., neighbor William Rosenberg saw dough to be made with his doughnut shop. Opened in 1950 as the Open Kettle, the lone shop proved more lucrative than the industrial-catering business Rosenberg had managed for years. After renaming the shop Dunkin' Donuts and buying out his partner, Rosenberg began franchising in 1955. Today, there are more than 3,500 outlets worldwide.

"I saw what [Johnson] was doing and thought it was such a good idea," Rosenberg once said to Nation's Restaurant News. "He became the impetus for me."

Across the country another entrepreneur was about to start the battle of the burger. Ray Kroc, a multimixer salesman from the Chicago area, was incredulous when he heard that a single hamburger stand in San Bernadino, Calif., was repeatedly ordering new multimixers to meet its milk-shake demand. In 1954 he decided to take a look for himself.

From the parking lot of McDonald's Famous Hamburgers, Kroc saw a vision that changed his life. For two days he watched doves of people approach the various windows of the eight-sided building to order 15-cent hamburgers, 10-cent fries and 20-cent shakes. Neatly dressed employees efficiently dispensed the products, allowing new customers to quickly step up.

The gold mine belonged to Richard and Maurice "Mac" McDonald, two brothers from New Hampshire who had traveled west during the Depression to strike it rich. After trying their hand at a series of other jobs, the brothers opened a small food stand at Santa Anita Racetrack in

Arcadia, Calif., in 1937. For 11 years they fine-tuned their concept before unveiling the now-infamous San Bernadino restaurant capable of serving 40 burgers every 100 seconds.

To better compete with the growing number of eateries lining the roadsides, the McDonalds also had crafted for the restaurant a distinct appearance. In addition to delicious burgers and fries, patrons were lured by an eye-catching red-and-white-tiled building in an octagonal shape. It was flanked by twin arches enhanced with neon.

Struck by the operation, Kroc sought out the McDonalds in search of his piece of the action. If the brothers would grow the chain, then he could sell more multimixers, he reasoned. But the brothers refused. Over the years they had already sold 21 franchises -- of which nine were operating -- and they were quite content with their already upscale lifestyle. Shortly thereafter, however, their sole franchisee retired. In 1955 Kroc gave birth to the McDonald's System Inc.

McDonald's eventually would become notable for its size, its marketing savvy and its "billions and billions" of burgers sold. But its true contribution to the evolution of franchising is slightly less obvious. According to Southwest Missouri's Dicke, Kroc and his colleagues would foment the development of the outlet as the product.

"The customer shifted," Dicke states. "McDonald's sells hamburger stands and Howard Johnson was selling clams."

Success Spawns Fraud

Concepts like KFC, Howard Johnson's, Dunkin' Donuts, McDonald's and myriad others spread like wildfire. Six years after its formation McDonald's had 228 units. Within eight years of its founding Dunkin' Donuts had 100 units. And by the time KFC reached its ninth anniversary it had 600 units.

During the 1960s Wall Street also took numerous franchise companies public, raising millions of dollars for investors. In Howard Johnson's first day of trading in 1960 the stock jumped from $38 to $52. Similarly, the day in 1965 that McDonald's stock was made available to the public it climbed from $22.50 to $30. Dunkin' Donuts made its offering debut in 1968. That same year KFC stock was trading at $90. Euphoria abounded, and the public was deluged with a steady stream of articles touting the joys of franchising.

In "Roadside Empires," Luxenberg writes: "In 1969, a group of Harvard Business School students reported that 40,000 people a year were purchasing franchises, and 90 percent of the new operators were surviving. The figures were alluring indeed."

It is not surprising that the apparent panacea attracted the dishonest as well as the honest. As more and more people turned to franchising as a way to rise from rags to riches, more and more bogus schemes surfaced. Charismatic characters found throngs of wide-eyed followers eager for their share of franchising's pot of gold. By the 1970s, pyramid schemes proliferated.

Almost a decade earlier in 1960 Dunkin' Donuts founder Rosenberg was struck with the idea to found a franchise association. He was attending a "Start Your Own Business Show" and recalled hearing complaint upon complaint about the rapidly changing industry. Because of more questionable operations, government officials were beginning to intervene.

"I'd never heard so much bitching in my life," Rosenberg recounts. So he and his peers anted up some money, created an agenda and elected officers. As envisioned, the group would promote and protect franchising interests from both the shadier figures giving the industry a bad name and the burgeoning attempts by government officials to regulate it.

"He founded it because franchisors could not get their ads into The Wall Street Journal until they cleaned up their act," Bill Cherkasky, who recently retired from the International Franchise Association, once recalled to Nation's Restaurant News. "He founded it as a protective organization ... and to make sure people viewed franchising as a clean business.

Government Steps In

Since the inception of the International Franchise Association it has had its hands full. During the 1970s state and federal officials began scrutinizing the industry full throttle. Congress held hearings, and several state attorneys general pursued their own investigations. Meanwhile, chains like Chicken Delight gave them fodder.

Founded in 1952, Chicken Delight had made its founder, A.L Tunick, a tidy sum by the time it was sold to Consolidated Foods in 1965. Within seven years 800 franchise holders were suing the company. According to Luxenberg in "Roadside Empires," "They had grown tired of paying inflated prices for supplies, providing the company with huge profits. A federal court sympathized with the franchisees, and Consolidated Foods sold its right to the Chicken Delight trademark, having concluded that without the old arrangement on supplies the company was no longer worth holding."

In response to similar episodes, several states began enacting disclosure requirements to ensure that prospective franchisees understood the systems they were entering. California blazed the trail in 1971 when its Legislature passed a franchise investment law. Fifteen more states would follow suit in time. In 1979 -- eight years of study -- the Federal Trade Commission joined in the effort to protect franchise investors. It promulgated federal regulations requiring franchisors to disclose designated information about their operations.

"People were promising the world, and it was not a well-regulated industry," Dicke of Southwest Missouri comments. "Part of the push came from franchisors themselves. It was one of those things where disclosure laws were in everybody's best interests."

The effectiveness of the FTC rule has been in question ever since it was put on the books, however. While franchise advocates appreciate its intention, they question almost all else about it.

"The good news was the FTC rule, for the first and only time, created a uniform minimum standard of franchise disclosure applicable to all franchise sales throughout the United States," Robert L. Purvin Jr., says in his 1994 book "The Franchise Fraud: How to Protect Yourself Before and After You Invest." "Without the rule in 35 states there would be no franchise sale protection whatsoever."

But there was bad news too, Purvin adds. As a practical matter, the FTC "had insufficient resources to monitor franchisor compliance or enforce the rule against violators," he says. He also points out that individuals still lacked the ability to bring private lawsuits if they are damaged by violations of the rule -- a fact that many franchisee advocates declare still needs to be addressed.

Furthermore, Purvin and others have pointed out that the FTC rule actually may do prospective franchisees a great disservice by creating the illusion that the federal government is regulating the industry closely. FTC officials themselves over the years have admitted a lack of resources to do a thorough job.

A Big Fight in the Heartland

As states were adding disclosure laws to their books, several also began addressing the franchisor-franchisee relationship. Although 17 states now have such laws on their books, it was the passage of the Iowa Franchise Act in 1992 that ushered in a new era dedicated to a familiar-but-somehow-lost philosophy: cooperation.

Initiated by KFC franchisees pitted against their franchisor in the aforementioned seven-year legal battle over their contracts, the legislation sought to spare franchise holders from abusive franchisor practices. The bill touched on several of the hot-button issues that continue to plague franchising, including encroachment, transfer, sourcing, nonrenewal and termination. To the dismay of franchisors, it found strong support in the Iowa Legislature.

Franchisors immediately embarked on an ongoing effort to have the law repealed or changed. Lawsuits and lobbying have, separately, shown some parts of the law to be unconstitutional and some parts to need amending. In 1995 lawmakers made some changes. Another reform bill now awaits Senate action.

It is not surprising that franchisors and franchisees find different meaning in what happened in Iowa. For some franchisors and their advocates it became a fight for survival.

"It was the first time a legislative body superimposed its will on the business contract," says Matthew R. Shay, vice president of government and regulatory affairs and chief counsel for the International Franchise Association, which opposed the law's passage. "They said, 'We know your business better than you do and therefore we, the Legislature, are going to establish the terms of the contract.'"

Franchisees and their advocates maintain that what sets Iowa apart is not the content of the law, but the mere fact that franchisees were able to coalesce their forces and get the law passed.

"I think [franchisors] were offended that the grassroots efforts were so successful in '92," remarks Brent Appel, a Des Moines, Iowa, attorney who helped pass the law. "In fact, the Iowa law is not much different from those in 17 other states. But they hope to prevent any other franchisee-rights statutes from enactment."

Regardless, the events in Iowa did serve to raise the clout of franchises. Two national franchisee groups -- the American Association of Franchisees and Dealers and the American Franchisee Association -- blossomed. And franchisors, afraid that other states might follow Iowa's lead and aware that Capitol Hill was starting to watch, welcomed back a commitment to working together. The IFA, after 33 years of catering to franchisors only, opened its doors to some franchisee members in 1993. Words like "partnership" and "mediation" became franchisor buzzwords.

Attempts to pass relationship in the years since have and by federal lawmakers in the years since have failed. But many franchisee advocates remain committed both to winning franchisees a private right of action and to establishing standards of conduct for franchisors. Rep John J. LaFalce, D-N.Y., who spearheaded congressional hearings into franchisor practices in the early 1990s, introduced another such measure in November 1997.

"Franchising is a very imbalanced relationship in which all of the qualifications and money is presumably on the franchisor side," says Harold Brown, a Boston attorney, author and longtime franchisee advocate. "The franchisee is helpless, even if he has a lot of money, because he doesn't know what's really going on. As I thought 27 years ago, the dominant party owes the obligation of good faith and fair dealing to the subservient party. Many state statutes and many court decisions agree with what I've told you, but some of the giants still fight it."

Despite the imblances so glaring to franchisee advocates, franchising remains both an awesome force in the economy and a happy lifestyle for many of the franchisees who enter into it.

A poll conducted in 1996 by Franchise Times, a franchise trade publication, found that 73 percent of more than 1,000 franchisees surveyed would recommend franchising to others. Meanwhile, 75 percent described themselves as very or somewhat satisfied and cited such reasons as independece, growth opportunities, high earnings and job security for their satisfaction. Incidentally, less that 3 percent mentioned franchisor support as a reason for satisfaction.

"I think franchising represents a very interesting blend of big business with entrepreneurship," states Jeffrey Bradach, assistant professor of organizational behavior at Harvard Business School in Cambridge, Mass. "...In different places this thing is growing fast, and I think it's because it has the characteristic of blending the benefits of scale with local entrepreneurship if it's managed well. When you go out and talk with franchisees, these are independent business people."

And while the franchisor-franchisee relationship has endured many twists and turns through the decades, Bradach suggests that it really hasn't changed much from the days when Harman and Sanders exchanged their handshake.

"Yes, it's become more litigious in some ways on both sides," he says. "But I would argue that the franchise systems that are very effective are built on strong relationships."

He adds, "The underlying dynamics of success, I don't think have changed. The minute things start referring to the contracts, the whole thing's already gone down the tubes."

CHAPTER–7

DIETICIANS AND CALORIES INTAKE

A dietitian is an expert in food and nutrition. Dietitians help promote good health through proper eating. They supervise the preparation and service of food, develop modified diets, participate in research, and educate individuals and groups on good nutritional habits. In a medical setting, a dietitian may provide specific artificial nutritional needs to patients unable to consume food normally. Dietary modification to address medical issues involving dietary intake is also a major part of dietetics. The goals of the dietary department are to provide medical nutritional intervention, obtain, prepare, and serve flavorsome, attractive, and nutritious food to patients, family members, and health care providers.

In many countries only people who have specified educational credentials can call themselves "dietitians" — the title is legally protected. The term "nutritionist" is also widely used; however, the term nutritionist is *not* regulated, and is not an accurate term to give to a dietitian. People may call themselves nutritionists without the educational and professional requirements of registered dietitians. A nutritionist is not a dietitian, as a dietitian is registered to a national board and accredited and a nutritionist is neither.

Different professional terms are used in different countries. Dietitians are valuable members of the medical multi-disciplinary team providing nutritional knowledge and acting as consultants to other health care professionals.

TYPES OF DIETITIANS

They work with other health care professionals and community groups to provide nourishment, nutritional programs and instructional presentations to benefit people of all ages, and with a variety of health conditions. This is accomplished by developing individual plans to meet nutritional needs.

These plans include nourishment, tube feedings (called enteral nutrition), intravenous feedings (called parenteral nutrition) such as total parenteral nutrition (TPN) or peripheral parenteral nutrition (PPN), diets, and education. Clinical dietitians provide individual and group educational programs for patients and family members about their nutrition and health.

Dietitians in Practice

Clinical Dietitians

Clinical dietitians work in hospitals and other health care facilities to provide nutrition therapy to patients according to the disease processes, provide individual dietary consultations to patients and their family members and also conduct group educations for other health workers, patients and the public. They coordinate both medical records and nutritional needs to assess the patients and make a plan based on their findings.

Some clinical dietitians have dual responsibilities with medical nutrition therapy and in food service, described below. In addition, clinical dietitians in smaller facilities will also provide or create outpatient education programs. They work as a team with the physicians, physician assistants, physical therapists, occupational therapists, pharmacists, speech therapists, social workers, nurses, Dietetic Technicians, and Volunteers to provide care to the patients.

Community Dietitians

Community dietitians work with wellness programs and international health organizations. These dietitians apply and distribute knowledge about food and nutrition to specific life-styles and geographic areas. They coordinate nutritional programs in public health agencies, daycare centers, health clubs, and recreational camps and resorts.

Some community dietitians carry out clinical based patient care in the form of home visits for patients who are too physically ill to attend consultation in health facilities.

Food Service Dietitians

Food service dietitians or managers are responsible for large-scale food planning and service. They coordinate, assess and plan food service processes in health care facilities, school food service programs, prisons, cafeterias and restaurants.

These dietitians will also perform audits of their departments, train other food service workers and use marketing skills to launch new menus and various programs within their institution. They direct and manage the operational and nutrition services staffs such as kitchen staffs, delivery staffs and dietary assistants or diet aides.

Gerontological Dietitians

Gerontological dietitians are specialist in nutrition and aging. They are Board certified in Gerontological Nutrition with the American Dietetic Association. They work in government agencies in aging policy, and in a regulatory capacity in the oversight of nursing homes and community-based care facilities. They work as Consultants in Nursing Homes, and in higher education in the field of Gerontology (the study of Aging.)

Pediatric Dietitians

Pediatric dietitians provide health advice for people under the age of 18.

Research Dietitians

Research dietitians are mostly involved with dietary related research in the clinical aspect of nutrition in disease states, public aspect on primary, secondary and sometimes tertiary health prevention and food service aspect in issues involving the food prepared for patients. Many registered dietitians also work with the biochemical aspects of nutrient interaction within the body. Research Dietitians normally work in a hospital or university research facilities. It should be noted that some Clinical dietitian's roles also involve research other than the normal clinical workload. Quality improvement in dietetics services is also one area of research.

Administrative Dietitians

The Administrator, manager, or director of a dietetics department or nutrition services program acts as head of the dietitians. They also hire, train, direct and supervise employees and manage dietary departments. Administrative dietitians may also apply procedure and policy as part of their management job.

Business Dietitians

Business dietitians serve as resource people for the media. Dietitians' expertise in nutrition is often taped for

TV, radio, and newspapers—either as an expert guest opinion, regular columnist or guest, or for resource, restaurant, or recipe development and critique.

Dietitians have served as show hosts on major television stations and as drive-time radio news anchors. Dietitians write books, appear on television cooking channels, and author corporate newsletters on nutrition and wellness. They also work as sales representatives for food manufacturing companies that provide nutritional supplements and tube feeding supplies.

Consultant Dietitians

Consultant dietitians work under private practice. The title 'consultant' in this case should not be confused with the identical title given to certain medical doctors in countries such as the United Kingdom and Ireland. The term consultant in this instance is synonymous with the title attending as used in countries such as the United States. Consultant dietitians contract independently to provide nutrition services and educational programs to individuals, nursing homes, and in health care facilities.

As recent studies have shown the importance of diet in both preventing and managing disease, many US states have moved towards covering medical nutrition therapy under the Medicaid/Medicare making consulting a much more lucrative option for dietitians due to insurance reimbursement.

OTHER NUTRITION PERSONNEL

These designations apply principally to the US although the generic classifications are likely to be applicable elsewhere.

Registered Dietetic Technicians (DTR)

Dietetic Technicians, Registered (DTR), possess a specialized Associate Degree from Community College programs which are accredited by the Commission on Accreditation of Dietetics Education (CADE) of the American Dietetic Association. Quite often, they work alongside Registered Dietitians, and like Registered Dietitians, they have in-depth knowledge of nutrition and food service. They must complete a dietetic internship with a minimum of 450 supervised practice hours in the areas of Food Service Theory and Management, Community Dietetics, and Clinical Dietetics.

They must also successfully pass a national registration examination administered by the Commission on Dietetic Registration (CDR) of the ADA. The DTR is an ADA credentialed nutrition practitioner who works independently in many nutrition settings, similar to the RD; however, when performing clinical dietetics, they must work under the supervision of a Registered Dietitian. Some states have current legislation specifying the scope of practice for the DTR in medical nutrition therapy settings.

Effective June 1, 2009, a new pathway to becoming a Registered Dietetic Technician has been made available by the Commission on Dietetic Registration. Students may take the DTR examination without attending an internship after completion of a Baccalaureate degree granted by a US regionally accredited college/university, or foreign equivalent, and completion of a Commission on Accreditation of Dietetics Education (CADE) Didactic Program in Dietetics (DPD) or Coordinated Program in Dietetics (CP). Applicants must take and pass the CDR Dietetic Technician Registration Exam to qualify for the DTR credential.

In the United States, the predominant and most respected Dietetics and Nutrition Education Organization is The American Dietetic Association (ADA). The ADA confers both the RD and DTR credentials, and the qualifications for such licensure is strict. In many cases, the ability to represent oneself as a "Dietitian" or "Dietetic Technician" is regulated by individual states. For instance, the California Business and Professions Code Section 2585-2586.8, states that:

2585. (a) Any person representing himself or herself as a registered dietitian *shall meet one of the following qualifications:* (1) Been granted, prior to January 1, 1981, the right to use the term "registered dietitian" by a public or private agency or institution recognized by the State Department of Health Services as qualified to grant the title, provided that person continues to meet all requirements and qualifications periodically prescribed by the agency or institution for the maintenance of that title. (2) *Possess all of the following qualifications:* (A) Be 18 years of age or older. (B) Satisfactory completion of appropriate academic requirements for the field of dietetics and related disciplines and receipt of a baccalaureate or higher degree from a college or university accredited by the Western Association of Schools and Colleges or other regional accreditation agency. (C) Satisfactory completion of a program of supervised practice for a minimum of 900 hours that is designed to prepare entry level practitioners through instruction and assignments in a clinical setting. Supervisors of the program shall meet minimum qualifications established by public or private agencies or institutions recognized by the State Department of Health Services to establish those qualifications. (D) Satisfactory completion of an examination administered by a public or private agency or institution recognized by the State Department of Health Services as qualified to administer the examinations. (E) Satisfactory completion of continuing education requirements established by a public or private agency or institution recognized by the State Department of Health Services to establish the requirements.

(b) *Any person representing himself or herself as a dietetic* technician, registered shall possess all of the following qualifications: (1) Be 18 years of age or older. (2) Satisfactory completion of appropriate academic requirements and receipt of an associate's degree or higher from a college or university accredited by the Western Association of Schools and Colleges or other regional accreditation agency. (3) Satisfactory completion of the dietetic technician program requirements by an accredited public or private agency or institution recognized by the State Department of Health Services including not less than 450 hours of supervised practice. (4) Satisfactory completion of an examination administered by a public or private agency or institution recognized by the State Department of Health Services to administer the examination. (5) Satisfactory completion of continuing education requirements established by a public or private agency or institution recognized by the State Department of Health Services to establish the requirements.

(c) It is a misdemeanor for any person not meeting the criteria of subdivision (a) or (b) to use, in connection with his or her name or place of business, the words "dietetic technician, registered," "dietitian," "dietician," "registered dietitian," "registered dietician," or the letters "RD," "DTR," or any other words, letters, abbreviations, or insignia indicating or implying that the person is a dietitian, or dietetic technician, registered or registered dietitian, or to represent, in any way, orally, in writing, in print or by sign, directly or by implication, that he or she is a dietitian or a dietetic technician, registered or a registered dietitian.

Dietary Assistants or Dietary Aides

Are responsible for assisting and carrying out the medical nutrition therapy prescribed by the Dietitians, and delegated by Registered Dietetic Technicians or Certified Dietary Managers. They are to ensure that food for the patients as instructed by their superiors are carried out correctly by checking menus against recent diet orders before tray assembly begins and being physically present in the kitchen plating-lines at meal hours. Dietary aides in some countries might also carry out a simple initial health screening for newly admitted patients and only inform the Dietitians if any screened patients requires a dietitian's expertise for further assessments or interventions.

Dietary Clerks

Dietary clerks perform clerical tasks such as entry and maintenance of dietary requirements to a database. They also track financial information, such as the number of meals served each day.

CERTIFIED DIETARY MANAGERS

Certified Dietary Managers are responsible for retail, catering and tray lines. If an operation is large, there may be one or more managers to help in directing the dietary workers. Certified Dietary Managers are certified by the credentialing agency known as the "Dietary Managers Association", or (DMA). This agency certifies not only Dietary Managers, but also another professional known as a Certified Food Protection Professional (CFPP). The DMA certifies specific programs to meet its educational requirements, and requires the programs to include courses in Culinary Management, Clinical Nutrition, and Food Safety. In addition, there are supervised practice requirements and a certification exam that must be passed. Certification through the Dietary Managers Association is respected in the Food service Industry.

Dietary Workers

Dietary workers prepare the food and meal trays in the kitchen. They check for accuracy and completeness. They also maintain the storage area for food supplies and ensure practice of sanitary procedures. Dietary workers are trained on the job and can work in any commercial kitchen.

Dietary Hosts

Dietary hosts or *hostesses* deliver and bring back the meal trays to patients. They distribute and collect menus and help the patients to make complete selections.

Required Qualifications and Professional Associations

A dietitian's education in health science involves significant scientific based knowledge in anatomy, chemistry, biochemistry, biology, physiology, nutrition, and medical science. In addition to this scientific instruction, dietitians must undergo an internship to learn counseling skills and aspects of psychology.

There are a few different academic routes to becoming a fully qualified registrable dietitian:

- A professional bachelor degree in Dietetics which requires four years of studies

or

- A bachelor of science degree and a postgraduate diploma in Dietetics

or

- A bachelor of science degree and a master's degree in Dietetics

Internship is also essential to become a fully qualified Dietitian. The internship process differ in different countries.

USA

In the US nutrition professionals include the registered dietitian (RD) and the "dietetic technician, registered" (DTR). These terms, as well as simply dietitian, or "dietetic technician" are legally protected terms regulated by the American Dietetic Association (ADA).

Dietitians are registered with the Commission on Dietetic Registration (the certifying agency of the ADA) and are only able to use the label "Registered Dietitian" when they have met strict, specific educational and professional prerequisites and passed a national registration examination.

Besides academic education, registered dietitians must complete at least 1200 hours of practical, supervised experience through an accredited program before they can sit for the registration examination. In a coordinated program (CP) students acquire internship hours concurrently with their coursework. In a didactic program (DP) these hours are obtained through a dietetic internship that is completed after obtaining a degree.

In both programs the student is required to complete several areas of competency including rotations in clinical, community, long-term care nutrition as well as food service, public health and a variety of other worksites.

Once the degree is earned, the internship completed, and registration examination passed, the individual can now use the nationally recognized legal term, Registered Dietitian and is able to work in a variety of professional settings. Most states require additional licensure to work in most settings. To maintain the RD credential, professionals must participate in and earn continuing education units (often 75 hours every 5 years.)

Canada

In the United States and Canada the Dietitian, Registered Dietitian (RD), etc. are similarly protected titles. The professional association in Canada is the Dietitians of Canada. The US equivalent of it is American Dietetic Association.

In Canada, each province has an independent professional college (for example, The College of Dietitians of Ontario) which is responsible for protecting the public and regulating the profession. The colleges are entirely funded from licensing fees collected from dietitians. Each college must have both public and professional members, and is empowered to investigate and censure (when malpractice/negligence is found) members of the profession who breach either their scope of practice or harm/endanger the health of a patient/client, and receive a complaint against them from a member of the public or another health care professional. To practice as a registered dietitian within a province, a dietitian must register with the college and obtain a license. The activities of the college are governed by legislation passed by the provincial government. It is the presence of this regulatory body which distinguishes registered dietitians from nutritionists in Canada.

In Canada, the colleges also set the minimum entry requirements for admission into practice as a registered dietitian. Requirements to entry into practice as a dietitian include a four year undergraduate degree from an accredited university (which includes courses in science, foods, nutrition, management, communication and psychology/sociology, among others), a 10 - 12 month supervised practice period (called an internship) and successfully passing a board exam in nutrition and dietetics.

Australia

Accredited Practising Dietitians (APDs) in Australia gain their qualifications through university courses accredited by the DAA (Dietitians Association of Australia). In order for patients to receive a rebate from Medicare or Private Health insurance APD status is required. APDs are Dietitians engaged in the Continuing Professional Development program offered by the DAA and commit to uphold the DAA Code of Professional Conduct and Code of Ethics.

Dietitians who do not wish to join the DAA may participate in the DAA's Continuing Professional Development Program without being a member of the DAA and in this way can still hold APD status. However, under new rules (which commenced 1 July 2009), health care providers must either have statutory registration or be members of their national professional association to obtain a provider number. This means all private health funds will require private practitioners applying for provider numbers to be DAA members (not just 'eligible' for membership).

International Confederation of Dietetic Associations (ICDA)

The International Confederation of Dietetic Associations is an organization of national associations of Dietitians and Nutritionists. Dietetics associations are professional societies whose members have education qualifications in food, nutrition and dietetics recognized by a national authority. Dietitians and Nutritionists are widely recognized as health professionals who promote health through food and nutrition.

ICDA supports national dietetics associations and their members, beyond national and regional boundaries, by providing:

- An integrated communications system
- An enhanced image for the profession
- Increased awareness of standards of education, training and practice in dietetics

CALORIE RESTRICTION

Caloric restriction (CR), or calorie restriction, is a dietary regimen that restricts calorie intake, where the baseline for the restriction varies, usually being the previous, unrestricted, intake of the subjects. Calorie restriction without malnutrition has been shown to improve age-related health and to slow the aging process in a wide range of animals and some fungi.

CR is one of the few dietary interventions that have been documented to increase both the median and maximum lifespan in a variety of species, among them yeast, fish, rodents and dogs. There are currently ongoing studies to investigate whether CR works in nonhuman primates, and its effects on human health and metabolic parameters associated with CR in other species. The results so far are positive, but the studies are not yet complete, due to the long lifespan of the species.

Research History

In 1934, Mary Crowell and Clive McCay of Cornell University observed that laboratory rats fed a severely reduced calorie diet while maintaining micronutrient levels resulted in life spans of up to twice as long as otherwise expected. These findings were explored in detail by a series of experiments with mice conducted by Roy Walford and his student Richard Weindruch. In 1986, Weindruch reported that restricting the calorie intake of laboratory mice proportionally increased their life span compared to a group of mice with a normal diet. The calorie-restricted mice also maintained youthful appearances and activity levels longer and showed delays in age-related diseases. The results of the many experiments by Walford and Weindruch were summarized in their book The Retardation of Aging and Disease by Dietary Restriction (1988) (ISBN 0-398-05496-7).

The findings have since been accepted and generalized to a range of other animals. Researchers are investigating the possibility of parallel physiological links in humans. In the meantime, many people have independently adopted the practice of calorie restriction in some form.

Effects of a Diet

A small study of long-term CR practitioners studied the effects of a diet with 10-25% less calorie intake than the average "Western" diet. Mean Body mass index (BMI) was 19.6 in the CR group; the matched group BMI was 25.9, comparable to the BMI for middle-aged people in the US.

The mean BMI in the CR group dropped from 24 (range of 19.4 to 29.6) to 19.5 (range of 16.5 to 22.8) over periods of 3–15 years. Nearly all the decrease in both BMI and cardiovascular risk factors occurred in the first year. Adjusting for age, the average total cholesterol and LDL (bad) cholesterol levels in the CR group were below those seen in all but the lowest 10% of the population. The average HDL (good) cholesterol levels were in the 85th to 90th percentile range for normal middle-aged US men.

The calorie-restricted group also fared much better than the control group in terms of average blood pressure (100/60 vs. 130/80 mm Hg), fasting glucose, fasting insulin (65% reduction), body mass index (19.6 ± 1.9 vs. 25.9 ± 3.2 kg/m^2), body fat percentage (8.7% ± 7% vs. 24% ± 8%), C-reactive protein, carotid IMT (40% reduction), and platelet-derived growth factor AB.

The CR group had triglyceride levels as low as the lowest 5% of Americans in their 20s. (The CR group age-range was 35-82.) Both systolic and diastolic blood pressure levels in the CR group were about 100/60, a level more typical of 10-year-olds. Fasting plasma insulin concentration was 65% lower. Fasting plasma glucose concentration was also lower.

The principal investigator in this study noted an apparent lower rate of cardiovascular aging, with arteriosclerosis progress indicators particularly slowed.

The comparison group's statistics aligned approximately with the US national average on the dimensions considered. Fasting plasma insulin levels and fasting plasma glucose levels are used as tests to predict diabetes.

The American CALERIE study began in 2007 and investigates the effects of a 25% reduction in calorie intake on healthy adults over a period of two years. The effect of CR on IGF-1 serum levels seen in rodents appears to only manifest in humans when protein intake is not much higher than the Recommended Dietary Allowance

Improved Memory

A 2009 research paper showed that a calorie restricted diet can improve memory in normal to overweight elderly. The diet also resulted in decreased insulin levels and reduced signs of inflammation. Scientists believe that memory improvement in this experiment was caused by the lower insulin levels, because high insulin levels are usually associated with lower memory and cognitive function. However, that relation seems to be age-specific since another study, when analyzing people older than 65, those who were underweight had a higher dementia risk than normal or overweight people.

Health Concerns

Although studies show that calorie restriction can improve longevity and health in model organisms, and studies in humans demonstrate reduced risk factors for major diseases, the long term effects of calorie restriction on humans are still unknown. In addition to a number of benefits, short-term studies of calorie restriction in humans have reported effects such as loss of muscle mass, muscle strength and reduced bone mineral density.

In some epidemiological studies, low body weight is associated with increased mortality, particularly in late middle-aged or elderly subjects. One study that received a great deal of media attention found that having a BMI lower than 18, for women, is associated with significantly increased mortality from noncancer, non"cardiovascular disease causes. The reasons for such results are unclear, and are often confounded by factors such as cigarette smoking and failure to exclude pre-existing disease.

The authors of this study attempted to adjust for these confounders, but other scientists argued that their methods for doing so were inadequate. "Over the subsequent weeks, epidemiologists from the ACS [American Cancer Society], American Heart Association, Harvard School of Public Health, and other organizations raised specific methodologic questions about the recent CDC study and presented analyses of other data sets. The main concern ... is that it did not adequately account for weight loss from serious illnesses such as cancer and heart disease ... and failed to account adequately for the effect of smoking on weight ... As a result, the Flegal study underestimated the risks from obesity and overestimated the risks of leanness."

Such results may be the result of "reverse causation," in which the causal relationship between two closely associated phenomena is mistakenly taken to be the reverse of what it actually is: thinness in older adults is often the result of medical conditions that themselves cause weight loss (such as cancer, chronic obstructive pulmonary disorder, or depression) or of the cachexia (wasting syndrome) and sarcopenia (loss of muscle mass, structure, and function) of aging.

In any case, epidemiological studies of body weight are not studies of calorie restriction as used in anti-aging studies. Indeed, they are not in fact studies of calorie intake to begin with, as body weight is influenced by many factors other than energy intake. Moreover, "the quality of the diets consumed by the low-BMI individuals are difficult to assess, and may lack nutrients important to longevity."

Indeed, typical low-calorie diets rarely provide the high nutrient intakes that are a necessary feature of an anti-aging calorie restriction diet. , , Moreover, "The lower-weight individuals in the studies are not CR because their caloric intake reflects their individual ad libitum set-points, and not a reduction from that set-point."

Concerns are sometimes raised that calorie restriction can make individuals feel hungry all the time and this may lead to them getting obsessed with food which can easily become the cause of various eating disorders. However, a controlled study of human calorie restriction found no increase in eating disorder symptoms or other harmful psychological effects, in line with extensive earlier research. In those who already suffer from a binge-eating disorder, calorie restriction can precipitate an episode of binge eating, but it does not seem to pose any such risk otherwise.

The effect of these diets on people who want to lose weight is controversial. Although calorie restriction may provide quick weight loss, several studies have shown that the body adjusts to the new diet in more or less half a year. Researchers argue that people who have little body fat should not use this method of losing weight but rather should exercise more because calorie restriction in this case can be harmful. The reason for this is that after the body's fat reserves have been burned for energy, the proteins within muscle tissue will be consumed. In severe cases where individuals do not acknowledge the dangers they are exposing themselves to, they may suffer serious loss of the muscle mass.

Several studies conducted in this sense revealed that dieters who restricted calories for 12 months had lower muscle mass and a reduced capacity to perform exercise compared with those who lost similar amounts of weight from exercise alone. Another study concluded that individuals who lost weight with the help of the calorie restriction diets are more prone to develop a loss of bone at the level of hip and spine, the area most at risk for bone fractures. Some specialists however claim that minor mineral losses can be prevented with supplements of vitamin D and calcium.

It has also been noted that people who are willing to lose weight by following such diets put themselves at risk of developing cold sensitivity, menstrual irregularities and even infertility and hormonal changes. Moreover, recent studies attack the earlier studies that found that calorie restriction may improve memory and attention. A study published in 2007 in Rejuvenation Research magazine shows that there is no significant link between this diet and memory or attention problems. Excessive calorie restriction may lead to swelling in the individual's legs and feet.

Especially in children, adolescents and young adults (under approximately 21), calorie restriction is not advised because this type of diet may interfere with the natural physical growth, as it has been observed in laboratory animals. In addition, mental development and physical changes to the brain take place in late adolescence and early adulthood that could be negatively affected by calorie restriction. Pregnant women are recommended not to try losing weight with this method. It has been shown that a low BMI is a risk factor in pregnancy as it may result in ovulatory dysfunction (infertility), and mothers who are underweight are more prone to preterm delivery.

Some specialists believe that calorie restriction may slow the healing time of the wounds which may have great impacts on the individual's overall health in case of hazard accidents or surgery.

Moreover, calorie restriction has been reported in mice to hinder their ability to fight infection, and some evidence suggests that in patients with amyotrophic lateral sclerosis calorie restriction accelerates the onset of the disease.

Individuals who are willing to lose weight with a calorie restriction diet of less than 1,500 calories a day need to be monitored by a specialist in order to prevent potential side effects.

Starvation

Severe calorie restriction may result in starvation, unless metabolism is also slowed by some means. The concept of a reduced calorie diet should not be confused with anorexia nervosa or other eating disorders. If such a pattern is repeated for prolonged periods of severe caloric restriction, the body may burn lean tissue (including but not limited to muscle and collagen) along with its remaining fat reserves. The combination of starvation and the associated lethargy and decreased physical activity can result in muscular atrophy which leads to lower quality of life.

Beyond using lean tissue as energy source, the presence of catabolic hormones, such as cortisol, and lack of anabolic ones, such as insulin, disrupts protein synthesis, amino acid uptake and weakens the immune system. It is possible that even moderate calorie restriction may be harmful in specific patient populations, such as lean persons who have minimal amounts of body fat.

EFFECTS OF CR ON DIFFERENT ORGANISMS

Primates

A study on rhesus macaques, funded by the National Institute on Aging, was started in 1989 at the University of Wisconsin–Madison and is still ongoing. This study has so far shown that caloric restriction in rhesus monkeys blunts aging and significantly delays the onset of age related disorders such as cancer, diabetes, cardiovascular disease and brain atrophy. The monkeys were enrolled in the study at ages of between 7 and 14 years; at the 20 year point 80% of the calorically restricted monkeys were still alive, compared to only half of the controls. These results bore out earlier preliminary results that showed lower fasting insulin and glucose levels as well as higher insulin sensitivity and LDL profiles associated with lower risk of atherogenesis in dietary restricted animals.

The most recent study conducted by Ricki J. Colman and Richard Weindruch at the University of Wisconsin used rhesus monkeys that live an average of 27 years and a maximum of 40, found that the dieting monkeys show many beneficial signs of caloric resistance, including significantly less diabetes, cancer, and heart and brain disease. However, as some of the monkeys are expected to live another 20 years, the findings are still inconclusive.

Results to date have found a trend toward a reduced overall death rate, which has not yet reached statistical significance. An additional analysis, restricted to causes of death related to aging, did find a significant reduction in age-related deaths. However, the interpretation of this finding is uncertain, as it is hypothetically possible exclusion of deaths due to non-aging causes may somehow mask an involvement of CR in such deaths. although the sample size is too low to say for certain.

Researchers at New York's Mount Sinai School of Medicine reported in 2006 that compared to monkeys fed a normal diet, squirrel monkeys on a life-long calorie-restrictive diet were less likely to develop Alzheimer's-like changes in their brains. Since squirrel monkeys are relatively long-lived, definitive conclusions regarding whether or not they are aging slower are not yet available.

Moderate CR attenuates age-related sarcopenia in primates.

Rodents

Seventy years ago, McCay CM, *et al.*, discovered that reducing the amount of calories fed to rodents nearly doubled their lifespans. The life extension was varied for each species but on average, there was a 30-40% increase in lifespan in both mice and rats. CR preserves a range of structural and functional parameters in aging rodents. For example, studies in female mice have shown that estrogen receptor-alpha declines in the aging pre-optic hypothalamus. The female mice that were given a calorically restricted diet during the majority of their lives maintained higher levels of ERá in the pre-optic hypothalamus than their non-calorically restricted counterparts.

Studies in female mice have shown that both Supraoptic nucleus (SON) and Paraventricular nucleus (PVN) lose about one-third of IGF-1R immunoreactivity with normal aging. Old calorically restricted (CR) mice lose higher numbers of IGF-1R non-immunoreactive cells while maintaining similar counts of IGF-1R immunoreactive cells in comparison to Old-Al mice. Consequently, Old-CR mice show a higher percentage of IGF-1R immunoreactive cells reflecting increased hypothalamic sensitivity to IGF-1 in comparison to normally aging mice.

Yeast

Fungi model are very easy to manipulate and many crucial steps toward the understanding of aging has been done with it. Many studies were published in budding yeast and fission yeast to analyse the cellular mechanisms behind the increased longevity due to calorie restriction.

First, calorie restriction is often called dietary restriction because the same effects on life span can be reached by only changing the nutrient quality without changing the amount of calories. The data from Dr Guarente, Dr Kennedy, Dr Jazwinski, Dr Kaeberlein, Dr Longo, Dr Shadel, Dr Nyström, Dr Piper and others showed that genetic manipulations in nutrient signaling pathways could mimic the effects of dietary restriction.

In some case dietary restriction needs mitochondrial respiration to increase longevity (chronological aging) and in some other case not (replicative aging). Nutrient sensing in yeast controls stress defense, mitochondrial functions, Sir2 and others. These functions are all known to regulate aging. Genes involved in these mechanisms are : TOR, PKA, SCH9, MSN2/4, RIM15, SIR2,...

Drosophila

Research in 2003 by Mair et al. showed that calorie restriction extends the life of fruit flies of any age with instantaneous effects on death rates.

Caenorhabditis Elegans

Recent work in *Caenorhabditis elegans* has shown that restriction of glucose metabolism extends life span by primarily increasing oxidative stress to exert an ultimately increased resistance against oxidative stress, a process called (mito)hormesis.

Mechanism of Action

Even though there has been research on CR for over 70 years the mechanism by which CR works is still not well understood. Some explanations included reduced cellular divisions, lower metabolism rates, reduced production of free radicals and hormesis.

Hormesis

Research has pointed toward hormesis as an explanation. Southam and Ehrlich (1943) reported that a bark extract that was known to inhibit fungal growth, actually stimulated growth when given at very low concentrations. They coined the term "hormesis" to describe such beneficial actions resulting from the response of an organism to a low-intensity biological stressor. The word "hormesis" is derived from the Greek word "hormaein" which means "to excite". The (Mito)hormesis hypothesis of CR proposes that the diet imposes a low-intensity biological stress on the organism, which elicits a defense response that helps protect it against the causes of aging. In other words, CR places the organism in a defensive state so that it can survive adversity, and this results in improved health and longer life. This switch to a defensive state may be controlled by longevity genes.

Mitochondrial Hormesis

The mitochondrial hormesis was a purely hypothetical concept until late 2007 when work by Michael Ristow's group in a small worm named Caenorhabditis elegans suggests that restriction of glucose metabolism extends life span primarily by increasing oxidative stress to stimulate the organism into having an ultimately increased resistance to further oxidative stress. This is probably the first experimental evidence for hormesis being the reason for extended life span following CR.

Although aging can be conceptualized as the accumulation of damage, the more recent determination that free radicals participate in intracellular signaling has made the categorical equation of their effects with "damage" more problematic than was commonly appreciated in years past. It was previously proposed on a hypothetical basis that free radicals may induce an endogenous response culminating in more effective adaptations which protect against exogenous radicals (and possibly other toxic compounds). Recent experimental evidence strongly suggests that this is indeed the case, and that such induction of endogenous free radical production extends life span of a model organism and mitohormetically exerts life extending and health promoting effects. Sublethal mitochondrial stress with an attendant stoichiometric augmentation of reactive oxygen species may precipitate many of the beneficial alterations in cellular physiology produced by caloric restriction.

Evolution

It has been recently argued that during years of famine, it may be evolutionarily desirable for an organism to avoid reproduction and to upregulate protective and repair enzyme mechanisms to try to ensure that it is fit for reproduction in future years. This seems to be supported by recent work studying hormones. A study in male mice has found that CR generally feminizes gene expression and many of the most significantly changed individual genes are involved in aging, hormone signaling, and p53-associated regulation of the cell cycle and apoptosis, it concluded that CR's life-extension effects might arise partly from a shift toward a gene expression profile more typical of females. Prolonged severe CR lowers total serum and free testosterone while increasing SHBG concentrations in humans, these effects are independent of adiposity.

Lowering of the concentration of insulin and substances which are related to insulin, e.g. Insulin-like growth factor 1 and Growth hormone has been shown to upregulate autophagy, the repair mechanism of the cell. A related hypothesis suggests that CR works by decreasing insulin levels and thereby upregulating autophagy, but CR affects many other health indicators and whether insulin is the main concern is still undecided. Calorie restriction has been shown to increase DHEA in primates, however it has not been shown to increase DHEA in post-pubescent primates. The extent to which these findings apply to humans is still under investigation.

Chromatin and PHA-4

Evidence suggests that the biological effects of CR are closely related to chromatin function. A study conducted by the Salk Institute for Biological Studies and published in the journal *Nature* in May 2007 determined that the gene PHA-4 is responsible for the longevity behind calorie restriction in roundworms, "with similar results expected in humans".

Free Radicals and Glycation

Two very prominent proposed explanations of aging which have a bearing on calorie restriction are the free radical theory and the glycation theory. With high amounts of energy available, mitochondria do not operate very efficiently and generate more superoxide. With CR, energy is conserved and there is less free radical generation. A CR organism will have less fat and require less energy to support the weight, which also means that there does not need to be as much glucose in the bloodstream. Less blood glucose means less glycation of adjacent proteins and less fat to oxidize in the bloodstream to cause sticky blocks resulting in atherosclerosis. Type II Diabetics are people with insulin insensitivity caused by long-term exposure to high blood glucose. Obesity leads to type 2 diabetes. Type 2 diabetes and uncontrolled type 1 diabetes are much like "accelerated aging", due to the above effects. There may even be a continuum between CR and the metabolic syndrome.

Calorie Restriction with Optimal Nutrition has not been tested in comparison to Calorie Excess with Optimal Nutrition. It may be that with extra calories, nutrition must be similarly increased to ratios comparable to that of Calorie Restriction to provide similar antiaging benefits. Stated levels of calorie needs may be biased towards sedentary individuals. Calorie restriction may be no more than adapting the diet to the body's needs.

Caloric Restriction Mimetics

Work on the mechanisms of CR has given hope to the synthesising of future drugs to increase the human lifespan by simulating the effects of calorie restriction. However, MIT biologist Leonard Guarente cautioned that "(treatment) won't be a substitute for a healthy lifestyle. You'll still need to go to the gym". Sir2 or "silent information regulator 2" is a sirtuin, discovered in baker's yeast cells, which is hypothesized to suppress DNA instability. In mammals Sir2 is known as SIRT1. David Sinclair at Harvard Medical School, Boston is a leading proponent of the view that the gene Sir2 may underlie the effect of calorie restriction in mammals by protecting cells from dying under stress. It is suggested a low-calorie diet that requires less Nicotinamide adenine dinucleotide to metabolize may allow SIRT1 to be more active in its life-extending processes. An article in the June 2004 issue of the journal *Nature* showed that SIRT1 releases fat from storage cells.

Sir2/SIRT1 and Resveratrol

Attempts are being made to develop CR mimetics interventions. Resveratrol has been reported to activate

Sir2/SIRT1 and extend the lifespan of yeast, nematode worms, fruit flies, and mice consuming a high caloric diet. Resveratrol does not extend lifespan in normal mice. The effect of resveratrol on lifespan in C. elegans and Drosophila was re-investigated by D. Gems and L. Partridge, they concluded previously reported lifespan increases were in fact due to natural variability in C. elegans lifespans A recent study found resveratrol extends the lifespan of a vertebrate fish by 59%. In the yeast, worm, and fly studies, resveratrol did not extend lifespan if the Sir2 gene was mutated. A 2010 study concluded that SRT1720 (and resveratrol are not direct activators of SIRT1. Matt Kaeberlein and Brian Kennedy at the University of Washington Seattle believe that Sinclair's work on resveratrol is an artifact and that the Sir2 gene has no relevance to CR, they have proposed that the caloric restriction increases lifespan by decreasing the activity of the Target of Rapamycin (TOR) kinase.

Gurarente has recently published that behavior associated with caloric restriction did not occur when Sirt1 knockout mice were put on a calorie restricted diet, the implication being that Sirt1 is necessary for mediating the effects of caloric restriction. However, the same paper also reported that the biochemical parameters thought to mediate the lifespan extending effects of calorie restriction (reduced insulin, igf1 and fasting glucose), were no different in normal mice and mice lacking Sirt1. Whether the lifespan-extending effect of CR was still evident in Sirt1 knockout mice was not reported in that study. According to Sinclair's data, Sirtuins (SirT1, Sir2, ...) are behind the putative effect of calorie restriction on longevity, however some research has cast doubt on this. A clinical trial of the resveratrol formulation SRT501 was suspended.

Objections

No Benefit to Houseflies, Overfed Model Organisms

One set of experiments shows that CR has no benefits in the housefly. The authors hypothesize that the widely purported effects of CR may be because a diet containing more calories can increase bacterial proliferation, or that the type of high calorie diets used in past experiments have a stickiness, general composition, or texture that reduces longevity.

Another related theory says that some of the calorie-restriction effects are artifacts, because the laboratory model organisms are kept at non-physiological high calorie diets. This would mean that calorie restriction simply means mimicking a natural environment energy supply.

Catabolic Damage

A major conflict with calorie restriction is that adequate calorie intake is needed to prevent catabolizing the body's tissues. A body in a catabolic state promotes the degeneration of muscle tissue, including the heart.

Physical Activity Testing Biases

While some tests of calorie restriction have shown increased muscle tissue in the calorie-restricted test subjects, how this has occurred is unknown. Muscle tissue grows when stimulated, so it is possible that the calorie-restricted test animals exercised more than their companions on higher calories. The reasons behind this may be that animals enter a foraging state during calorie restriction. In order to control this variable, such tests would need to be monitored to make sure that levels of physical activity are equal between groups.

Insufficient Calories and Amino Acids for Exercise

Exercise has also been shown to increase health and lifespan and lower the incidence of several diseases. Calorie restriction comes into conflict with the high calorie needs of athletes, and may not provide them adequate levels of energy or sufficient amino acids for repair, although this is not a criticism of CR per se, since it is certainly possible to be an unhealthy athlete, or an athlete destined to die at a young age due to poor diet, stresses, etc. Moreover, in experiments comparing CR to exercise, CR animals live much longer than exercised animals.

Does Calorie Restriction only Benefit the Young?

There is some evidence to suggest that the benefit of CR in rats might only be reaped in early years. A study on rats which were gradually introduced to a CR lifestyle at 18 months showed no improvement over the average lifespan of the Ad libitum group. This view, however, is disputed by Spindler, Dhahbi, and colleagues who showed that in late adulthood, acute CR partially or completely reversed age-related alterations of liver, brain and heart proteins and that mice placed on CR at 19 months of age show increases in lifespan. The Wisconsin rhesus monkey study showed increased survival rates and decreased diseases of aging from caloric restriction even though the study started with adult monkeys.

Midlife Onset of Calorie Restriction as a Means of Prolonging Lifespan

This is a highly controversial topic of if and how to start such in Midlife in humans. See the books by lifetime calorie restriction research Roy Walford which offer inconclusive but supportive evidence for this thesis.

Possible Contraindications

Both animal and human research suggest BUD CR may be contraindicated for people with amyotrophic lateral sclerosis (ALS). Research on a transgenic mouse model of ALS demonstrates that CR may hasten the onset of death in ALS. Hamadeh *et al.* therefore concluded: "These results suggest that CR diet is not a protective strategy for patients with amyotrophic lateral sclerosis (ALS) and hence is contraindicated." Hamadeh *et al.* also note two human studies that they indicate show "low energy intake correlates with death in people with ALS." However, in the first study, Slowie, Paige, and Antel state: "The reduction in energy intake by ALS patients did not correlate with the proximity of death but rather was a consistent aspect of the illness." They go on to conclude: "We conclude that ALS patients have a chronically deficient intake of energy and recommended augmentation of energy intake." (PMID 8604660)

Previously, Pedersen and Mattson also found that in the ALS mouse model, CR "accelerates the clinical course" of the disease and had no benefits. Suggesting that a calorically dense diet may slow ALS, a ketogenic diet in the ALS mouse model has been shown to slow the progress of disease. More recently, Mattson *et al.* opine that the death by ALS of Roy Walford, a pioneer in CR research and its antiaging effects, may have been a result of his own practice of CR. However, as Mattson *et al.* acknowledge, Walford's single case is an anecdote that by itself is insufficient to establish the proposed cause-effect relation.

Negligible Effect on Larger Organisms

Another objection to CR as an advisable lifestyle for humans is the claim that the physiological mechanisms that determine longevity are very complex, and that the effect would be small to negligible in our species.

Intermittent Fasting as an Alternative Approach

Studies by Mark P. Mattson, Ph. D., chief of the National Institute on Aging's (NIA) Laboratory of

Neurosciences, and colleagues have found that intermittent fasting and calorie restriction affect the progression of diseases similar to Huntington's disease, Parkinson's disease, and Alzheimer's disease in mice (PMID 11119686). In one study, rats and mice ate a low-calorie diet or were deprived of food for 24 hours every other day (PMID 12724520). Both methods improved glucose metabolism, increased insulin sensitivity, and increased stress resistance. Researchers have long been aware that calorie restriction extends lifespan, but this study showed that improved glucose metabolism also protects neurons in experimental models of Parkinson's and stroke.

Another NIA study found that intermittent fasting and calorie restriction delays the onset of Huntington's disease-like symptoms in mice and prolongs their lives (PMID 12589027). Huntington's disease (HD), a genetic disorder, results from neuronal degeneration in the striatum. This neurodegeneration results in difficulties with movements that include walking, speaking, eating, and swallowing. People with Huntington's also exhibit an abnormal, diabetes-like metabolism that causes them to lose weight progressively.

This NIA study compared adult HD mice who ate as much as they wanted with HD mice who were kept on an intermittent fasting diet during adulthood. HD mice possess the abnormal human gene huntingtin and exhibit clinical signs of the disease, including abnormal metabolism and neurodegeneration in the striatum. The mice on the fasting program developed clinical signs of the disease about 12 days later and lived 10 to 15% longer than the free-fed mice.

The brains of the fasting mice also showed less degeneration. Those on the fasting program also regulated their glucose levels better and did not lose weight as quickly as the other mice. Researchers found that fasting mice had higher brain-derived neurotrophic factor (BDNF) levels. BDNF protects neurons and stimulates their growth. Fasting mice also had high levels of heat-shock protein-70 (Hsp70), which increases cellular resistance to stress.

Another NIA study compared intermittent fasting with cutting calorie intake. Researchers let a control group of mice eat freely (ad libitum). Another group was fed 60% of the calories that the control group consumed. A third group was fasted for 24 hours, then permitted to free-feed. The fasting mice didn't cut total calories at the beginning and the end of the observation period, and only slightly cut calories in between.

A fourth group was fed the average daily intake of the fasting mice every day. Both the fasting mice and those on a restricted diet had significantly lower blood sugar and insulin levels than the free-fed controls. Kainic acid, a toxin that damages neurons, was injected into the dorsal hippocampus of all mice.

Hippocampal damage is associated with Alzheimer's. Interestingly, the scientists found less damage in the brains of the fasting mice than in those that ate a restricted diet, and most damage in mice with an unrestricted diet. But the control group which ate the average daily intake of the fasting mice also showed less damage than the mice with restricted diet.

Another Mattson study in which overweight adult asthmatics followed alternate day calorie restriction (ADCR) for eight weeks showed marked improvement in oxidative stress, inflammation, and severity of the disease. Evidence from the medical literature suggests that ADCR in the absence of weight loss prolongs lifespan in humans. Intermittent fasting has also been shown to increase the resistance of neurons in the brain to excitotoxic stress.

DAILY CALORIE INTAKE

In the contemporary times, people are becoming very calorie conscious. Well, calories are like a must for the body, as it is the calories that the human body burns in order to produce energy. But as it said that excess of anything is bad, same applies to the intake of calories too. If there is an excess of calories in our body, it gets stored in the form of fats, thus making us overweight.

Adult calorie requirement differs from that of a child and in the same ways the daily calorie requirement of an athlete would be distinct from that of a person who doesn't have a very active routine because his entire day goes away sitting in the front of computer, doing desk job. Thus, the calorie intake requirement differs from person to person, depending upon several factors like age, body composition and level of physical activity on a daily basis and many more.

The general recommendation as far as the calorie intake is concerned is that men need about 2700 calories per day and women require about 2000 calories per day. But these recommendations are suggested for average body structure adults, who perform their usual day-to-day activities and do not follow a vigorous workout.

It is suggested by dieticians that your calorie intake should be such that 50 to 60% of the total calorie intake is contributed by carbohydrates, 20% by proteins and 15 to 20% should come from fat. It is advisable for expectant mothers to consume 300 extra calories per day, whereas lactating mothers require about 550 calories at the initial level and at gradual levels, their calorie intake should be about 400 calories per day. Well, as vital are calories for the body, equally important is to burn the extra calories through an active fitness workout.

CHAPTER–8

TOP FOOD SERVICES COMPANIES: A CASE STUDY

The food service industry is made up of restaurants, catering companies and food distributors. Essentially, the industry encompasses any meal made outside of the home. Since the industry has such a variety of companies, the three largest companies (by revenue) in the industry are highlighted in this article.

SYSCO CORPORATION

The Sysco Corporation is the largest food service distributor in the world. The company's revenue is about $37 billion, and it has more than 100 different distribution centers in the world. Sysco distributes food and equipment to colleges, hospitals, schools and restaurants around the world. In fact, Sysco was ranked the No. 1 company in the Wholesale Food and Grocery Division by "Fortune" magazine in 2006.

U.S. Food Service

U.S. Food service is the second-largest food service distributor in the world. The company distributes food and utensils to restaurants, health care facilities and educational institutions. In addition, the company also works with managers of the companies it distributes to on a number of things such as food safety, promotions and trends in the food industry.

U.S. Food service Headquarters

9755 Patuxent Woods Drive

Columbia, MD 21046-2286

United States

410-312-7100

usfood service.com

Yum Brands

Yum Brands is the largest restaurant company in the world. The company has more than 37,000 restaurants in 110 countries. In 2009, Yum Brands had revenues exceeding $11 billion. The company's restaurant brands include Taco Bell, Kentucky Fried Chicken, Long John Silver's, Pizza Hut, A&W Restaurants and Wing Street.

KFC

KFC primarily sells chicken pieces, wraps, salads and sandwiches. While its primary focus is fried chicken, KFC also offers a line of grilled and roasted chicken products, side dishes and desserts. Outside North America, KFC offers beef based products such as hamburgers or kebabs, pork based products such as ribs and other regional fare.

The company was founded as Kentucky Fried Chicken by Colonel Harland Sanders in 1952, though the idea of KFC's fried chicken actually goes back to 1930. Although Sanders died in 1980, he remains an important part of the company's branding and advertisements, and "Colonel Sanders" or "The Colonel" is a metonym for the company itself. The company adopted KFC, an abbreviated form of its name, in 1991.

Starting in April 2007, the company began using its original name, Kentucky Fried Chicken, for its signage, packaging and advertisements in the U.S. as part of a new corporate re-branding program; newer and remodeled restaurants will have the new logo and name while older stores will continue to use the 1980s signage. Additionally, Yum! continues to use the abbreviated name freely in its advertising.

Born and raised in Henryville, Indiana, Sanders passed through several professions in his lifetime. Sanders first served his fried chicken in 1930 in the midst of the Great Depression at a gas station he owned in North Corbin, Kentucky. The dining area was named Sanders Court & Café and was so successful that in 1936 Kentucky Governor Ruby Laffoon granted Sanders the title of honorary *Kentucky Colonel* in recognition of his contribution to the state's cuisine. The following year Sanders expanded his restaurant to 142 seats, and added a motel he bought across the street. When Sanders prepared his chicken in his original restaurant in North Corbin, he prepared the chicken in an iron skillet, which took about 30 minutes to do, too long for a restaurant operation. In 1939, Sanders altered the cooking process for his fried chicken to use a pressure fryer, resulting in a greatly reduced cooking time comparable to that of deep frying. In 1940 Sanders devised what came to be known as his *Original Recipe*.

The Sanders Court & Café generally served travelers, often those headed to Florida, so when the route planned in the 1950s for what would become Interstate 75 bypassed Corbin, he sold his properties and traveled the U.S. to sell his chicken to restaurant owners. The first to take him up on the offer was Pete Harman in South Salt Lake, Utah; together, they opened the first "Kentucky Fried Chicken" outlet in 1952. By the early 1960s, Kentucky Fried Chicken was sold in over 600 franchised outlets in both the United States and Canada. One of the longest-lived franchisees of the older Col. Sanders' chicken concept, as opposed to the KFC chain, was the Kenny Kings chain. The company owned many Northern Ohio diner-style restaurants, the last of which closed in 2004.

Sanders sold the entire KFC franchising operation in 1964 for $2 million USD, equal to $14,161,464 today. Since that time, the chain has been sold three more times: to Heublein in 1971, to R.J. Reynolds in 1982 and most recently to PepsiCo in 1986, which made it part of its Tricon Global Restaurants division, which in turn was spun off in 1997, and has now been renamed to Yum! Brands.

In 2001, KFC started test in Austin, Texas restaurants of "Wing Works" chicken wing line sold with one of a few flavored sauces. Also, KFC hired a consultant to develop a breakfast menu.

Additionally, Colonel Sanders' nephew, Lee Cummings, took his own Kentucky Fried Chicken franchises (and a chicken recipe of his own) and converted them to his own "spin-off" restaurant chain, Lee's Famous Recipe Chicken.

Today, some of the older KFC restaurants have become famous in their own right. One such restaurant is located in Marietta, Georgia. This store is notable for a 56-foot (17 m) tall sign that looks like a chicken. The sign, known locally as the Big Chicken, was built for an earlier fast-food restaurant on the site called Johnny Reb's Chick, Chuck and Shake. It is often used as a travel reference point in the Atlanta area by locals and pilots.

The Secret Recipe

The Colonel's secret flavor recipe of 11 herbs and spices that creates the famous "finger lickin' good" chicken remains a trade secret. Portions of the secret spice mix are made at different locations in the United States, and the only complete, handwritten copy of the recipe is kept in a vault in corporate headquarters.

On September 9, 2008, the one complete copy was temporarily moved to an undisclosed location under extremely tight security while KFC revamped the security at its headquarters. Before the move, KFC disclosed that the recipe, which includes exact amounts of each component, is written in pencil on a single sheet of notebook paper and signed by Sanders. It was locked in a filing cabinet with two separate combination locks. The cabinet also included vials of each of the 11 herbs and spices used.

Only two unnamed executives had access to the recipe at any one time. One of the two executives said that no one had come close to guessing the contents of the secret recipe, and added that the actual recipe would include some surprises. On February 9, 2009, the secret recipe returned to KFC's Louisville headquarters in a more secure, computerized vault guarded by motion detectors and security cameras. Reportedly, the paper has yellowed and the handwriting is now faint.

In 1983, writer William Poundstone examined the recipe in his book *Big Secrets.* He reviewed Sanders' patent application, and advertised in college newspapers for present or former employees willing to share their knowledge. From the former he deduced that Sanders had diverged from other common fried-chicken recipes by varying the amount of oil used with the amount of chicken being cooked, and starting the cooking at a higher temperature (about 400 °F (200 °C)) for the first minute or so and then lowering it to 250 °F (120 °C) for the remainder of the cooking time.

Several of Poundstone's contacts also provided samples of the seasoning mix, and a food lab found that it consisted solely of sugar, flour, salt, black pepper and monosodium glutamate (MSG). He concluded that it was entirely possible that, in the years since Sanders sold the chain, later owners had begun skimping on the recipe to save costs. Following his buyout in 1964, Colonel Sanders himself expressed anger at such changes, saying:

That friggin' ... outfit .... They prostituted every goddamn thing I had. I had the greatest gravy in the world and those sons of bitches—they dragged it out and extended it and watered it down that I'm so goddamn mad!

Ron Douglas, author of the book *America's Most Wanted Recipes*, also claims to have figured out KFC's secret recipe.

Products

Packaging

The famous paper bucket that KFC uses for its larger sized orders of chicken and has come to signify the company was originally created by Wendy's restaurants founder Dave Thomas. Thomas was originally a franchisee of the original Kentucky Fried Chicken and operated several outlets in the Columbus, Ohio area. His reasoning behind using the paper packaging was that it helped keep the chicken crispy by wicking away excess moisture. Thomas was also responsible for the creation of the famous rotating bucket sign that came to be used at most KFC locations in the US.

Nutritional Value

KFC formerly used partially hydrogenated oil in its fried foods. This oil contains relatively high levels of trans fat, which increases the risk of heart disease. The Center for Science in the Public Interest (CSPI) filed a court case against KFC, with the aim of making it use other types of oils or make sure customers know about trans fat content immediately before they buy food.

In October 2006, KFC announced that it would begin frying its chicken in trans fat-free oil. This would also apply to their potato wedges and other fried foods, however, the biscuits, macaroni and cheese, and mashed potatoes would still contain trans fat.

Trans fat-free soybean oil was introduced in all KFC restaurants in the U.S. by April 30, 2007. CSPI announced that it would immediately drop its lawsuit against KFC and was hopeful that this would create a ripple effect on other restaurants or fast food chains that prepare food rich in trans fat. "If KFC, which deep-fries almost everything, can get the artificial trans fat out of its frying oil, anyone can," CSPI executive director Michael Jacobson said in a statement.

Advertising

Throughout the mid 1980s, KFC called on Will Vinton Studios to produce a series of humorous, claymation ads. These most often featured a cartoon-like chicken illustrating the poor food quality of competing food chains, mentioning prolonged freezing and other negative aspects. TV ads also featured Foghorn Leghorn advising Henry Hawk to visit the restaurant for better chicken.

In the 1980s, KFC was an associate sponsor for Junior Johnson's NASCAR Winston Cup Series cars, with such drivers as Darrell Waltrip, Neil Bonnett, and Terry Labonte.

A 1982 episode of *Little House on the Prairie* titled "Wave of the Future" featured a character presumed to be Col. Sanders offering Harriet Oleson a fried chicken franchise (perhaps a subliminal advertisement for KFC), but his character was credited as "Bearded Man" for legal reasons. This sub plot was an anacrhonism as Sanders had not yet been born at the time the episode was set (the late 19th century).

In 1997, KFC briefly re-entered the NASCAR Winston Cup Series as sponsor of the #26 Darrell Waltrip Motorsports Chevrolet with driver Rich Bickle at the Brickyard 400.

By the late 1990s, the stylized likeness of Colonel Sanders as the KFC logo had been modified. KFC ads began featuring an animated version of "the Colonel" voiced by Randy Quaid with a lively and enthusiastic attitude. He would often start out saying "The Colonel here!" and moved across the screen with a cane in hand. The Colonel was often shown dancing, singing, and knocking on the TV screen as he spoke to the viewer about the product.

The animated Colonel is uncommon today. Still using a humorous slant, the current KFC campaign revolves mostly around customers enjoying the food. It also features a modified version of Lynyrd Skynyrd's "Sweet Home Alabama" as the theme song for practically all its commercials, though the restaurant actually hails from Kentucky.

Many KFC locations are co-located with one or more of Yum! Brands restaurants, Long John Silver's, Taco Bell, Pizza Hut, or A&W Restaurants. Many of these locations behave like a single restaurant, offering a single menu with food items from both restaurants.

One of KFC's latest advertisements is a commercial advertising its "wicked crunch box meal". The commercial features a fictional black metal band called "Hellvetica" performing live, the lead singer then swallows fire. The commercial then shows the lead singer at a KFC eating the "wicked crunch box meal" and saying "Oh man that is hot".

In 2007, the original, non-acronymic *Kentucky Fried Chicken* name was resurrected and began to reappear on company marketing literature and food packaging, as well as some restaurant signage.

In 2010, an advertisement was shown in Australia showing an Australian cricket fan giving West Indies fans KFC chicken to keep them quiet. The ad sparked a debate over racism in the ad, suggesting that all black people eat fried chicken. Fried chicken was eaten by black slaves because it was cheap and easy to make. Though KFC stated that it was "misinterpreted by a segment of people in the US", the ad was later pulled from TV.

However, several Australian commentators have expressed the opinion that the ad is not racist, because this is not a racial stereotype in Australia and the cricket fans in the ad are not African American, but West Indies cricket supporters (the West Indies cricket team was playing a Test cricket series against the Australian cricket team at the time of the ad).

Also in 2010, Yum! signed a naming rights deal with the Louisville Arena Authority for Louisville's new downtown arena, which opened on October 10 of that year as the KFC Yum! Center.

PIZZA HUT

Pizza Hut is an American restaurant chain and international franchise that offers different styles of pizza along with side dishes including pasta, buffalo wings, breadsticks, and garlic bread.

Pizza Hut is a subsidiary of Yum! Brands, Inc. (the world's largest restaurant company) with approximately 34,000 restaurants, delivery/carry-out locations, and kiosks in 100 countries.

Concept and Format

Pizza Hut is split into several different restaurant formats; the original family-style dine-in locations; store front delivery and carry-out locations; and hybrid locations that offer carry-out, delivery, and dine-in options. Many full-size Pizza Hut locations offer *lunch buffet*, with "all-you-can-eat" pizza, salad, bread sticks, and a special pasta. Additionally, Pizza Hut also has a number of other business concepts that are different from the store type; Pizza Hut "Bistro" locations are "Red Roof's which offer an expanded menu and slightly more upscale options.

"Pizza Hut Express" and "The Hut" locations are fast food restaurants. They offer a limited menu with many products not found at traditional Pizza Huts. These type of stores are often paired in a colocated location with a sibling brand such as Wing Street, KFC or Taco Bell, and are also found on college campuses, food courts, theme parks, and in stores such as Target.

Traditionally, Pizza Hut has been known for its ambiance as much as pizza. Vintage "Red Roof" locations can be found throughout the United States, and quite a few exist in the UK and Australia. Even so, many such locations offer delivery/carryout service. This building style was common in the 1960s and 1970s.

The name "Red Roof" is somewhat anachronistic now, since many locations have brown roofs. Dozens of "Red Roofs" have closed or been relocated/rebuilt. Many "Red Roof" branches have beer if not a full bar, music from a jukebox, and sometimes an arcade. In the 1980s, the company moved into other successful formats including delivery/carryout and the fast food "Express" model.

The oldest continuously operating Pizza Hut in the world is in Manhattan, Kansas, in a shopping and tavern district known as Aggieville near Kansas State University.

Products

Pizza Hut sells "Stuffed Crust" pizza, with the outermost edge wrapped around a coil of mozzarella cheese; "Hand-Tossed," more like traditional pizzeria crusts; "Thin 'N Crispy", a thin, crispy dough which was

Pizza Hut's original style; "Dippin' Strips pizza", a pizza cut into small strips that can be dipped into a number of sauces; and "The Edge pizza," where the toppings nearly reach to the edge of the pizza. There was also formerly a crust that was not as thick as Pizza Hut's pan pizza, and not as thin as its thin crust. This crust was used on the Full House XL pizza and discontinued in 2007.

A new, upscale concept was unveiled in 2004, called Pizza Hut Italian Bistro. Unveiled at fifty locations nationwide, the Bistro is similar to a traditional Pizza Hut, except that new, Italian themed dishes are offered, such as penne pasta, chicken pomodoro, toasted sandwiches and other foods. Instead of black, white, and red, Bistro locations feature a burgundy and tan motif. Pizza Hut Bistros still serve the chain's traditional pizzas and sides as well. In some cases, Pizza Hut has replaced a "Red Roof" location with the new concept.

A new version of Pizza Hut pizza, named Pizza Mia which is lightly topped, was introduced in 2007. The product is aimed at the cost sensitive consumer segment and is priced similarly to the Domino's 555 deal, where each pizza is priced at five dollars if purchased in bulk of three or more. In comparison, a Pizza Hut medium sized, hand-tossed pepperoni pizza is internationally priced at $10.24 (Dallas, Texas 1/1/2009). The Pizza Mia comes in only one size (medium) and extra toppings range from $1.25 to $1.49. One slice of Pizza Hut pepperoni Pizza Mia weighs 83 grams, while one slice of Pizza Hut pepperoni hand-tossed pizza weighs 96 grams.

Pizza Hut on May 9, 2008, created and sold in Seattle, Denver, and Dallas, "The Natural", a new all-natural multi-grain crust sweetened with honey, a red sauce of organic tomatoes and topped all-natural cheese (or with all-natural chicken sausage and roasted red peppers). A medium Natural pizza with one topping sold for $9.99.

This was discontinued on October 27, 2009 in the Dallas market. It has since launched a nationwide advertising campaign. Also in 2008, Pizza Hut created their biggest pizza ever, the Panormous Pizza. Pizza Hut introduced the Big Eat Tiny Price Menu on June 21, 2009. It features new Pizza Rolls, the P'Zone Pizza, new Personal Panormous Pizza, and the Pizza Mia Pizza, each item starting at $5.00 or $5.99.

Pizza Hut introduced stuffed pan pizza on August 23, 2009 with $10.99 for one toppings and specialty for $13.99. Unlike regular stuffed crust cheese is not inside the crust, just pressed into the pan crust. Pizza Hut introduced the Big Italy, a pizza that is almost two feet long for $12.00, on August 22, 2010.

Pizza Hut recently (2010) came under fire when its supplier of palm oil, Sinar Mas, was exposed to be illegally slashing and burning the Paradise Forests of Indonesia to plant palm oil plantations. This act is driving native people off their land and forcing orangutans and Sumatran tigers to the brink of extinction.

Advertising

Pizza Hut's very first ad was "Putt Putt to Pizza Hut". It starts with a man apparently ordering take-out and driving his 1965 Mustang JR to Pizza Hut, while some of the townspeople start chasing him. He picks up his pizza and goes to his house, when all of the people who were chasing him start eating all the pizza except the man who ordered it. Frustrated, he calls Pizza Hut again.

Until early 2007, Pizza Hut's main advertising slogan was "Gather 'round the good stuff", and was "Now You're Eating!" from 2008 to 2009. The advertising slogan is currently "Your Favorites. Your Pizza Hut." Pizza Hut does not have an official international mascot, but at one time, there were commercials in the United States called 'The Pizza Head Show.' These commercials ran from 1993 to

1997 and were based loosely on the Mr. Bill shorts from *Saturday Night Live* in the 1970s.

The ads featured a slice of pizza with a face made out of toppings called 'Pizza Head'. In the 1970s Pizza Hut used the signature red roof with a jolly man named "Pizza Hut Pete". Pete was on the bags, cups, balloons and hand puppets for the kids. In Australia during the Mid to late 1990s, the advertising mascot was a delivery boy named Dougie, with boyish good looks who, upon delivering pizza to his father, would hear the catchphrase "Here's a tip: be good to your mother".

Pizza Hut sponsored the 1989 film *Back to the Future Part II*, and offered a free pair of futuristic sunglasses, known as "Solar Shades", with the purchase of Pizza Hut pizza. Pizza Hut also engaged in product placement within the film itself, having a futuristic version of their logo with their trademarked red hut printed on the side of a mylar dehydrated pizza wrapper in the McFly family dinner scene, and appear on a storefront in Hill Valley in the year 2015.

The 1990 NES game *Teenage Mutant Ninja Turtles II: The Arcade Game*, came with a coupon for a free pizza. The game was filled with Pizza Hut advertising and pizza that would refill the character's life.

In 1994, Donald Trump and ex-wife Ivana Trump starred in a commercial. The ending of the commercial showed Ivana Trump asking for the last slice, to which Donald replied, "Actually dear, you're only entitled to half", a play on the couple's recent divorce.

In 1995, Ringo Starr starred in a Pizza Hut commercial which also featured The Monkees. Rush Limbaugh also starred in a Pizza Hut commercial the same year, where he boasts that "nobody is more right than me," yet he states that for the first time he will do something wrong, which was to participate in Pizza Hut's then "eating pizza crust first" campaign regarding their stuffed crust pizzas.

Talk show host Jonathan Ross, co-starred in an ad with American model, Caprice Bourret. They were used to advertise the stuffed crust pizza, with Jonathan Ross saying "Stuffed Cwust", to which is a play on Jonathan's pronunciation of 'R's.

Another UK ad shows British Formula One driver Damon Hill visit a Pizza Hut restaurant and order a pizza, with famous F1 commentator Murray Walker visiting with him, and narrating as though it was a Formula One race. As Hill is about to finish his meal, Walker, in a play on Hill's 1994 & 1995 seasons where he was runner up in the Formula One World Championship both won by Michael Schumacher, shouts "And Hill finishes second, again!" at which Hill grabs Walker by his shirt and shakes him angrily, Walker proclaiming, in his usual tones, "He's lost it! He's out of control!"

Following England's defeat to Germany on penalties in the semi-finals of Euro 96, Gareth Southgate, Stuart Pearce and Chris Waddle featured in an advert. The advert shows Southgate wearing a paper bag over his head in shame as he was the one, who missed the crucial penalty against the Germans. Waddle and Pearce, who both missed penalty kicks in Italia 90 are ridiculing him, emphasising the word 'miss' at every opportunity. After Southgate finishes his pizza he takes off his paper bag, heads for the door and bangs his head against the wall. Pearce responds with, "this time he's hit the post".

In 1997, former Soviet Union Premier Mikhail Gorbachev starred in a Pizza Hut commercial to raise money for the Perestroyka Archives. In recent years, Pizza Hut has had various celebrity spokespeople, including Jessica Simpson, the Muppets, and Damon Hill and Murray Walker. Recent commercials have Queen Latifah providing the voiceover. Also in 1997, Pizza Hut, reunited "greatest of all time boxer" Muhammad Ali with trainer Angelo Dundee in a sentimental made for Super Bowl commercial.

In 1998 Pizza Hut paired with PlayStation character Crash from Crash Bandicoot: Warped which was later released that year.

Pizza Hut sponsored the first space pizza delivery in 2001 to the International Space Station (ISS), and paid for their logo to appear on a Russian Proton rocket in 2000, which launched the Russian Zvezda module.

In Australia, 2006 saw the introduction of a mascot in Pizza Hut's advertising – "Pizza Mutt", a small dog who delivers pizzas. The mascot was dumped after just two ads.

Early 2007 saw Pizza Hut move into several more interactive ways of marketing to the consumer. Utilizing mobile phone SMS technology and their MyHut ordering site, they aired several television commercials (commencing just before the Super Bowl) containing hidden words that viewers could type into their phones to receive coupons.

Other innovative efforts included their "MySpace Ted" campaign, which took advantage of the popularity of social networking, and the burgeoning user-submission marketing movement via their Vice President of Pizza contest.

Pizza Hut is also advertised in anime such as *Code Geass, Maria-sama ga Miteru, Darker Than Black* and *Toaru Kagaku no Railgun*, though in the translated versions of *Code Geass* the logo was removed, leaving only the red roof logo.

As of October 2009, Pizza Hut is advertising its WingStreet brand on a nationwide basis, having met its internal requirement of 80% of stores having the product available.

PASTA HUT

On April 1, 2008, Pizza Hut in America sent emails to customers advertising that they now offer pasta items on their menu. The email (and similar advertising on the company's website) stated "Pasta so good, we changed our name to Pasta Hut!"

The name change was a publicity stunt held in conjunction with April Fools' Day, extending through the month of April, with the company's Dallas headquarters changing its exterior logo to Pasta Hut. This name change was also used to promote the new Tuscani Pasta line and new Pizza Hut dine-in menu. The first Pasta Hut advertisement has the original Pizza Hut restaurant being imploded, and recreated with a sign saying "Pasta Hut" placed on the building.

United Kingdom

In the United Kingdom, Pizza Hut announced it would be changing its name to Pasta Hut in October 2008, six months after the US 'April Fool' trial. This was announced as being a temporary name change to reflect the chain's new emphasis on healthier foods On January 19, 2009, Pizza Hut announced that the Pasta Hut trial had ended and that the names of all stores previously converted to Pasta Hut would be converted back to Pizza Hut, following an online poll in which 81% chose to keep the Pizza Hut name.

Costa Rica

In Costa Rica, aside from the Pizza Hut restaurants, there is another brand called "PHD - Pizza Delivered Hot by Pizza Hut." This brand is only for food courts at malls and for express delivery. This was created to compete on the "fast food" market while restaurants will concentrate in casual food.

Book It!

Pizza Hut has been a longtime sponsor of the "Book It!" program (started in 1984), which encourages reading in American and Australian schools. Those who read books according to the goal set by the classroom teacher are rewarded with Pizza Hut coupons good for a free one-topping Personal Pan Pizza or discounted menu items. In the late 1980s, Pizza Hut threw free pizza parties for classes if all students met their reading goals.

The program has been criticized by some psychologists on the grounds that it may lead to overjustification and reduce children's intrinsic interest in reading. However, a study of the Pizza Hut program, Book It!, found that participation in the program neither increased nor decreased reading motivation. The program's 25th anniversary was in 2009. Book It! in Australia ceased in 2002 when Pizza Hut in Australia was removing its dine-in stores as Australians opt for take away pizza instead of dine-in.

Nutrition

In the UK, Pizza Hut has been criticized for the high salt content of its meals, some of which were found to contain more than twice the daily recommended amount of salt for an adult. The meats that consumers demand for pizza toppings (pepperoni, sausage, bacon, etc.) are, likewise, salty and fatty meats. There have also been concerns raised over food production practices as due to the high level of frozen produce being used.

CHAPTER–9

LAYOUT AND DESIGN IN PUBS AND BARS

By the end of the 18th century a new room in the pub was established: the saloon. Beer establishments had always provided entertainment of some sort — singing, gaming or a sport. Balls Pond Road in Islington was named after an establishment run by a Mr. Ball that had a pond at the rear filled with ducks, where drinkers could, for a certain fee, go out and take a potshot at shooting the fowl.

More common, however, was a card room or a billiards room. The saloon was a room where for an admission fee or a higher price of drinks, singing, dancing, drama or comedy was performed and drinks would be served at the table. From this came the popular music hall form of entertainment—a show consisting of a variety of acts.

A most famous London saloon was the Grecian Saloon in *The Eagle*, City Road, which is still famous these days because of an English nursery rhyme: "Up and down the City Road / In and out The Eagle / That's the way the money goes / Pop goes the weasel." The implication being that, having frequented the Eagle public house, the customer spent all his money, and thus needed to 'pawn' his 'weasel' to get some more. The exact definition of the 'weasel' is unclear but the two most likely definitions are: that a weasel is a flat iron used for finishing clothing;

or that 'weasel' is rhyming slang for a coat (*weasel and stoat*).

A few pubs have stage performances such as serious drama, stand-up comedy, musical bands or striptease; however juke boxes and other forms of pre-recorded music have otherwise replaced the musical tradition of a piano and singing.

PUBLIC BAR

By the 20th century, the saloon, or lounge bar, had settled into a middle-class room — carpets on the floor, cushions on the seats, and a penny or two on the prices, while the public bar, or tap room, remained working class with bare boards, sometimes with sawdust to absorb the spitting and spillages, hard bench seats, and cheap beer.

Later, the public bars gradually improved until sometimes almost the only difference was in the prices, so that customers could choose between economy and exclusivity (or youth and age, or a jukebox or dartboard). During the blurring of the class divisions in the 1960s and 1970s, the distinction between the saloon and the public bar was often seen as archaic, and was frequently abolished, usually by the removal of the dividing wall or partition itself. While the names of saloon and public bar may still be seen on the doors of pubs, the prices (and often the standard of furnishings and decoration) are the same throughout the premises, and many pubs now comprise one large room.

However, the modern importance of dining in pubs encourages some establishments to maintain distinct rooms or areas, especially where the building has the right characteristics for this. Yet, in a few pubs there still remain rooms or seats that, by local custom, "belong" to particular customers.

However there still remain a few, mainly city centre pubs, that retain a public bar mainly for working men that call in for a drink while still dressed in working clothes and dirty boots. They are now very much in a minority, but some landlords prefer to separate the manual workers from the better dressed businessmen or diners in the lounge or restaurant.

Snug

The "snug", also sometimes called the *Smoke room*, was typically a small, very private room with access to the bar that had a frosted glass external window, set above head height. A higher price was paid for beer in the snug and nobody could look in and see the drinkers. It was not only the well off visitors who would use these rooms, the snug was for patrons who preferred not to be seen in the public bar.

Ladies would often enjoy a private drink in the snug in a time when it was frowned upon for ladies to be in a pub. The local police officer would nip in for a quiet pint, the parish priest for his evening whisky, and lovers would use the snug for their rendezvous.

Counter

It was the public house that first introduced the concept of the bar counter being used to serve the beer. Until that time beer establishments used to bring the beer out to the table or benches. A bar might be provided for the manager to do his paperwork whilst keeping an eye on his customers, but the casks of ale were kept in a separate taproom. When the first public houses were built, the main room was the public room with a large serving bar copied from the gin houses, the idea being to serve the maximum number of people in the shortest possible time. It became known as the public bar.

The other, more private, rooms had no serving bar— they had the beer brought to them from the public bar. There are a number of pubs in the Midlands or the North which still retain this set up but these days the beer is fetched by the customer from the taproom or public bar.

One of these is The Vine, known locally as The Bull and Bladder, in Brierley Hill near Birmingham. In the Manchester district the public bar was known as the "vault", other rooms being the lounge and snug as usual elsewhere. By the early 1970s there was a tendency to change to one large drinking room and breweries were eager to invest in interior design and theming.

Isambard Kingdom Brunel, the British engineer and railway builder, introduced the idea of a circular bar into the Swindon station pub in order that customers were served quickly and didn't delay his trains. These island bars became popular as they also allowed staff to serve customers in several different rooms surrounding the bar.

Beer Engine

A "beer engine" is a device for pumping beer, originally manually operated and typically used to dispense beer from a cask or container in a pub's basement or cellar. It was invented by the locksmith and hydraulic engineer Joseph Bramah. Strictly the term refers to the pump itself, which is normally manually operated, though electrically powered and gas powered pumps are occasionally used; when manually powered, the term "handpump" is often used to refer to both the pump and the associated handle.

Pub Companies

After the development of the large London Porter breweries in the 18th century, the trend grew for pubs to become tied houses which could only sell beer from one brewery (a pub not tied in this way was called a Free house). The usual arrangement for a tied house was that the pub was owned by the brewery but rented out to a private individual (landlord) who ran it as a separate business (even though contracted to buy the beer from the brewery).

Another very common arrangement was (and is) for the landlord to own the premises (whether freehold or leasehold) independently of the brewer, but then to take a mortgage loan from a brewery, either to finance the purchase of the pub initially, or to refurbish it, and be required as a term of the loan to observe the solus tie.

A growing trend in the late 20th century was for breweries to run their pubs directly, using managers rather than tenants. Most such breweries, such as the regional brewery Shepherd Neame in Kent and Young's in London, control hundreds of pubs in a particular region of the UK, whilst a few, such as Greene King, are spread nationally. The landlord of a tied pub may be an employee of the brewery—in which case he would be a manager of a managed house, or a self-employed tenant who has entered into a lease agreement with a brewery, a condition of which is the legal obligation (trade tie) only to purchase that brewery's beer.

This tied agreement provides tenants with trade premises at a below market rent providing people with a low-cost entry into self-employment. The beer selection is mainly limited to beers brewed by that particular company. A Supply of Beer law, passed in 1989, was aimed at getting tied houses to offer at least one alternative beer, known as a guest beer, from another brewery. This law has now been repealed but while in force it dramatically altered the industry. Some pubs still offer a regularly-changing selection of guest beers.

The period since the 1980s saw many breweries absorbed by, or becoming by take-overs larger companies in the food, hotel or property sectors. The low returns of a pub-owning business led to many breweries selling their pub estates, especially those in cities, often to a new generation of small companies, many of which have now grown considerably and have a national presence. Other pub chains, such as *All Bar One* and *Slug and Lettuce* offer youth-oriented atmospheres, often in premises larger than traditional pubs.

Organisations such as Wetherspoons, Punch Taverns and O'Neill's, were formed in the UK since changes in legislation in the 1980s necessitated the break-up of many larger tied estates. A PubCo is a company involved in the retailing but not the manufacture of beverages, while a Pub chain may be run either by a PubCo or by a brewery.

Pubs within a chain will usually have items in common, such as fittings, promotions, ambience and range of food and drink on offer. A pub chain will position itself in the marketplace for a target audience. One company may run several pub chains aimed at different segments of the market. Pubs for use in a chain are bought and sold in large units, often from regional breweries which are then closed down. Newly acquired pubs are often renamed by the new owners, and many people resent the loss of traditional names, especially if their favourite regional beer disappears at the same time.

Brewery Tap

A brewery tap is the nearest outlet for a brewery's beers. This is usually a room or bar in the brewery itself, though the name may be applied to the nearest pub. The term is not applied to a brewpub which brews and sells its beer on the same premises.

PARTICULAR KINDS OF PUBS

Country Pubs

A "country pub" by tradition is a rural public house. However, the distinctive culture surrounding country pubs, that of functioning as a social centre for a village and rural community, has been changing over the last thirty or so years. In the past, many rural pubs provided opportunities for country folk to meet and exchange (often local) news, while others—especially those away from village centres—existed for the general purpose, before the advent of motor transport, of serving travellers as coaching inns.

In more recent years, however, many country pubs have either closed down, or have been converted to establishments intent on providing seating facilities for the consumption of food, rather than a venue for members of the local community meeting and convivially drinking.

Theme Pubs

Pubs that cater for a niche clientele, such as sports fans or people of certain nationalities are known as theme pubs. Examples of theme pubs include sports bars, rock pubs, biker pubs, Goth pubs, strip pubs, karaoke bars and Irish pubs.

In Canada and some other locations the majority of theme pubs are referred to as bars, such as 'biker bar', 'sports bar', 'gay bar', 'strip bar', 'Irish bar' etc. Pubs centred on dance floors featuring DJs or, less often, live music, are usually referred to as 'dance clubs'.

Signs

In 1393 King Richard II compelled landlords to erect signs outside their premises. The legislation stated "Whosoever shall brew ale in the town with intention of selling it must hang out a sign, otherwise he shall forfeit his ale." This was in order to make alehouses easily visible to passing inspectors, borough ale tasters, who would decide the quality of the ale they provided. William Shakespeare's father, John Shakespeare was one such inspector.

Another important factor was that during the Middle Ages a large proportion of the population would have been illiterate and so pictures on a sign were more useful than words as a means of identifying a public house. For this reason there was often no reason to write the establishment's name on the sign and inns opened without a formal written name, the name being derived later from the illustration on the public house's sign.

The earliest signs were often not painted but consisted, for example, of paraphernalia connected with the brewing process such as bunches of hops or brewing implements, which were suspended above the door of the public house. In some cases local nicknames, farming terms and puns were also used. Local events were also often commemorated in pub signs. Simple natural or religious symbols such as 'The Sun', 'The Star' and 'The Cross' were also incorporated into pub signs, sometimes being adapted to incorporate elements of the heraldry (e.g. the coat of arms) of the local lords who owned the lands upon which the public house stood. Some pubs also have Latin inscriptions.

Other subjects that lent themselves to visual depiction included the name of battles (e.g. Trafalgar), explorers, local notables, discoveries, sporting heroes and members of the royal family. Some pub signs are in the form of a pictorial pun or rebus. For example, a pub in Crowborough, East Sussex called *The Crow and Gate* has an image of a crow with gates as wings.

A British Pathe News film of 1956 shows artist Michael Farrar-Bell at work producing inn signs.

Most British pubs still have decorated signs hanging over their doors, and these retain their original function of enabling the identification of the public house. Today's pub signs almost always bear the name of the pub, both in words and in pictorial representation. The more remote country pubs often have stand-alone signs directing potential customers to their door.

Names

Pub names are used to identify and differentiate each public house. Modern names are sometimes a marketing ploy or attempt to create 'brand awareness', frequently using a comic theme thought to be memorable, *Slug and Lettuce* for a pub chain being an example. Interesting origins are not confined to old or traditional names, however. Names and their origins can be broken up into a relatively small number of categories.

As many public houses are centuries old, many of their early customers were unable to read, and pictorial signs could be readily recognised when lettering and words could not be read.

Pubs often have traditional names. A common name is the "Marquis of Granby". These pubs were named after John Manners, Marquess of Granby, who was the son of John Manners, 3rd Duke of Rutland and a general in the 18th century British Army. He showed a great concern for the welfare of his men, and on their retirement, provided funds for many of them to establish taverns, which were subsequently named after him.

Many names for pubs that appear nonsensical may have come from corruptions of old slogans or phrases, such as "The Bag o'Nails" (Bacchanals), "The Cat and the Fiddle" (Caton Fidèle) and "The Bull and Bush", which purportedly celebrates the victory of Henry VIII at "Boulogne Bouche" or Boulogne-sur-Mer Harbour.

Entertainment

Traditional games are played in pubs, ranging from the well-known darts, skittles, dominoes, cards and bar billiards, to the more obscure Aunt Sally, Nine Men's Morris and ringing the bull. In the UK betting is legally limited to certain games such as cribbage or dominoes, played for small stakes. In recent decades the game of pool (both the British and American versions) has increased in popularity as well as other table based games such as snooker or Table Football also becoming common.

Increasingly, more modern games such as video games and slot machines are provided. Many pubs also hold special events, from tournaments of the aforementioned games to karaoke nights to pub quizzes. Some play pop music and hip-hop (dance bar), or show football and rugby union on big screen televisions (sports bar). Shove ha'penny and Bat and trap were also popular in pubs south of London.

Many pubs in the UK also have football teams composed of regular customers. Many of these teams are in leagues that play matches on Sundays, hence the term "Sunday League Football". Bowling is also found in association with pubs in some parts of the country and the local team will play matches against teams invited from elsewhere on the pub's bowling green.

Pubs may be venues for pub songs and live music. During the 1970s pubs provided an outlet for a number of bands, such as Kilburn and the High Roads, Dr. Feelgood and The Kursaal Flyers, who formed a musical genre called Pub rock that was a precursor to Punk music.

Food

Pub Grub

Traditionally pubs in England were drinking establishments and little emphasis was placed on the serving of food, other than "bar snacks", such as pork scratchings, and pickled eggs, along with salted crisps and peanuts which helped to increase beer sales.

If a pub served meals they were usually basic cold dishes such as a ploughman's lunch. In South East England (especially London) it was common until recent times for vendors selling cockles, whelks, mussels and other shellfish, to sell to customers during the evening and at closing time. Many mobile shellfish stalls would set up near pubs, a practice that continues in London's East End.

In the 1950s some British pubs would offer "a pie and a pint", with hot individual steak and ale pies made easily on the premises by the landlord's wife. In the 1960s and 1970s this developed into the then-fashionable "chicken in a basket", a portion of roast chicken with chips, served on a napkin, in a wicker basket.

Quality dropped but variety increased with the introduction of microwave ovens and freezer food. "Pub grub" expanded to include British food items such as steak and ale pie, shepherd's pie, fish and chips, bangers and mash, Sunday roast, ploughman's lunch, and pasties. In addition, dishes such as burgers, lasagne and chilli con carne are often served.

Since the 1990s food has become more important as part of a pub's trade, and today most pubs serve lunches and dinners at the table in addition to (or instead of) snacks consumed at the bar. They may have a separate dining room. Some pubs serve meals to a higher standard, to match good restaurant standards; these are sometimes termed gastropubs.

Gastropub

A gastropub concentrates on quality food. The name is a combination of pub and gastronomy and was coined in 1991 when David Eyre and Mike Belben took over The Eagle pub in Clerkenwell, London. The concept of a restaurant in a pub reinvigorated both pub culture and British dining, though has occasionally attracted criticism for potentially removing the character of traditional pubs.

Records

Highest

The highest pub in the United Kingdom is the Tan Hill Inn, Yorkshire, at 1,732 feet (528 m) above sea level. The remotest pub on the British mainland is The Old Forge in the village of Inverie, Lochaber, Scotland. There is no road access and it may only be reached by an 18-mile (29 km) walk over mountains, or a 7-mile (11 km) sea crossing.

Likewise, the Berney Arms in Norfolk has no road access. It may be reached by foot or by boat, and also by train as it is served by the nearby Berney Arms railway station which likewise has no road access and serves no other settlement.

Smallest

Contenders for the smallest public house in the UK include :

- The Nutshell, Bury St Edmunds
- The Lakeside Inn, Southport
- The Little Gem, Aylesford, Kent
- The Smiths Arms, Godmanstone, Dorset
- The Signal Box Inn, Cleethorpes

The list includes a small number of parlour pubs, one of which is the Sun Inn, in Herefordshire.

Largest

The largest public house in the UK is The Moon Under Water, Manchester; as with many Wetherspoons it is in a converted cinema.

Oldest

A number of pubs claim to be the oldest surviving establishment in the United Kingdom, although in several cases original buildings have been demolished and replaced on the same site. Others are ancient buildings that saw uses other than as a pub during their history.

Ye Olde Fighting Cocks in St Albans, Hertfordshire, holds the Guinness World Record for the oldest pub in England, as it is an 11th century structure on an 8th century site. Ye Olde Trip To Jerusalem in Nottingham is claimed to be the "oldest inn in England". It has a claimed date of 1189, based on the fact it is constructed on the site of the Nottingham Castle brewhouse; the present building dates from around 1650.

Likewise, The Nags Head, Burntwood only dates back to the 16th century, but there has been a pub on the site since at least 1086, as it is mentioned in the Domesday Book. There is archaeological evidence that parts of the foundations of 'The Old Ferryboat Inn', Holywell, Cambridgeshire, may date to AD 460, and there is evidence of ale being served as early as AD 560.

The Bingley Arms, Leeds, is claimed to date to 905 AD. Ye Olde Salutation Inn in Nottingham dates from 1240, although the building served as a tannery and a private residence before becoming an inn sometime before the English Civil War. The Adam and Eve in Norwich was first recorded in 1249, when it was an alehouse for the workers constructing nearby Norwich Cathedral. Ye Olde Man & Scythe in Bolton is mentioned by name in a charter of 1251, but the current building is dated 1631. Its cellars are the only surviving part of the older structure.

CULTURAL ASSOCIATIONS

The highwayman Dick Turpin used the Swan Inn at Wroughton-on-the-Green in Buckinghamshire as his base. In the 1920s John Fothergill (1876-1957) was the innkeeper of the Spread Eagle in Thame, Berkshire, and published his autobiography: *An Innkeeper's Diary* (London: Chatto & Windus, 1931).

During his idiosyncratic occupancy many famous people came to stay, such as H. G. Wells. United States president George W. Bush fulfilled his lifetime ambition of visiting a 'genuine British pub' during his November 2003 state visit to the UK when he had lunch and a pint of non-alcoholic lager with British Prime Minister Tony Blair at the Dun Cow pub in Sedgefield, County Durham.

London

Many of London's pubs are known to have been used by famous people, but in some cases, such as the association between Samuel Johnson and Ye Olde Cheshire Cheese, this is speculative, based on little more than the fact that the person is known to have lived nearby. However, Charles Dickens is known to have visited the Cheshire Cheese, the Prospect of Whitby, Ye Olde Cock Tavern and many others. Samuel Pepys is also associated with the Prospect of Whitby and the Cock Tavern.

The Fitzroy Tavern is a public house situated at 16 Charlotte Street in the Fitzrovia district, to which it gives its name. It became famous (or according to others, infamous) during a period spanning the 1920s to the mid 1950s as a meeting place for many of London's artists, intellectuals and bohemians such as Dylan Thomas, Augustus John, and George Orwell. Several establishments in Soho, London, have associations with well-known, post-war literary and artistic figures, including the Pillars of Hercules, The Colony Room and the Coach and Horses. The Canonbury Tavern, Canonbury, was the prototype for Orwell's ideal English pub, *The Moon Under Water.*

The Red Lion in Parliament Square is close to the Palace of Westminster and is consequently used by political journalists and Members of Parliament. The pub is equipped with a Division bell that summons MPs back to the chamber when they are required to take part in a vote. The Punch Bowl, Mayfair was at one time jointly owned by Madonna and Guy Ritchie and is known for the number of present-day celebrities that have patronised it.

The Coleherne public house in Earls Court was a well-known gay pub from the 1950s. It attracted many well-known patrons, such as Freddie Mercury, Kenny Everett and Rudolph Nureyev. It was also used by the serial-killer Colin Ireland to pick-up victims.

In 1966 The Blind Beggar in Whitechapel became infamous as the scene of a murder committed by gangster Reggie Kray. The Ten Bells is associated with several of the victims of Jack the Ripper. In 1955, Ruth Ellis, the last woman executed in the United Kingdom, shot David Blakely as he emerged from *The Magdala* in South Hill Park, Hampstead, the bullet holes can still be seen in the walls outside. It is said that Vladimir Lenin and a young Joseph Stalin met in the *Crown and Anchor* pub (now known as *The Crown Tavern*) on Clerkenwell Green when the latter was visiting London in 1903.

The Angel, Islington was formerly a coaching inn, the first on the route northwards out of London, where Thomas Paine is believed to have written much of *The Rights of Man.* It was mentioned by Charles Dickens, became a Lyons Corner House, and is now a Co-operative

Bank. It is also on the board in the British version of the board game Monopoly.

OXFORD AND CAMBRIDGE

The Eagle and Child and the Lamb and Flag, Oxford, were regular meeting places of the Inklings, a writers' group which included J. R. R. Tolkien and C. S. Lewis. The Eagle in Cambridge is where Francis Crick interrupted patrons' lunchtime on 28 February 1953 to announce that he and James Watson had "discovered the secret of life" after they had come up with their proposal for the structure of DNA. The anecdote is related in Watson's book *The Double Helix*.

Television Soap Operas

The major soap operas on British television each feature a pub, and these pubs have become household names. The Rovers Return is the pub in *Coronation Street*, the British soap broadcast on ITV. The Queen Vic (short for the Queen Victoria) is the pub in *EastEnders*, the major soap on BBC One, while The Bull in the Radio 4 soap opera *The Archers* and the Woolpack in ITV's *Emmerdale* are also important meeting points. The sets of each of the three major television soap operas have been visited by some of the members of the royal family, including Queen Elizabeth II. The centrepiece of each visit was a trip into the Rovers, the Queen Vic, or the Woolpack to be offered a drink.

Pubs Outside Britain

Although "British" or "Irish" pubs found outside of Britain and its former colonies are often themed bars owing little to the original British public house, a number of "true" pubs may be found around the world.

In Denmark—a country, like Britain, with a long tradition of brewing—a number of pubs have opened which eschew "theming", and which instead focus on the business of providing carefully conditioned beer, often independent of any particular brewery or chain, in an environment which would not be unfamiliar to a British pub-goer. Some import British cask ale, rather than beer in kegs, in order to provide the full British real ale experience to their customers. This newly-established Danish interest in British cask beer and the British pub tradition is reflected by the fact that some 56 British cask beers were available at the 2008 European Beer Festival in Copenhagen, which was attended by more than 20,000 people.

In Ireland pubs are known for their atmosphere or "craic". In Irish, a pub is referred to as *teach tábhairne* ("tavernhouse") or *teach óil* ("drinkinghouse"). Live music, either sessions of traditional Irish music or varieties of modern popular music, is frequently featured in the pubs of Ireland. Pubs in Northern Ireland are largely identical to their counterparts in the Republic except for the lack of spirit grocers.

A side-effect of the 'Troubles' was that the lack of a tourist industry meant that a higher proportion of traditional bars have survived the wholesale refitting of Irish pub interiors in the English style in the 1950s and 1960s. This refitting was driven by the need to expand seating areas to accommodate the growing numbers of tourists, and was a direct consequence of the growing dependence of the Irish economy on tourism.

BAR

A bar is an establishment that serves alcoholic drinks — beer, wine, liquor, and cocktails — for consumption on the premises. Bars provide stools or chairs that are placed at tables or counters for their patrons. Some bars have entertainment on a stage, such as a live band, comedians, go-go dancers, or strippers.

Types of bars range from dive bars to elegant places of entertainment for the elite. Many bars have a happy hour to encourage off-peak patronage. Bars that fill to capacity sometimes implement a cover charge during their peak hours. Such bars often feature entertainment, which may be a live band or a popular disk jockey.

The term "bar" is derived from the specialized counter on which drinks are served. The "back bar" is a set of shelves of glasses and bottles behind that counter. In some establishments, the back bar is elaborately decorated with woodwork, etched glass, mirrors, and lights.

There have been many names throughout history for establishments where people gather to drink alcoholic beverages. Even when an establishment uses a different name, such as "tavern," the area of the establishment where the bartender serves alcoholic beverages is normally called "the bar."

There were prohibitions of alcoholic beverages in the first half of the 20th century in several countries, including Finland, Iceland, Norway, and the United States. In the United States, illegal bars during Prohibition were called speakeasies or blind pigs.

Legal Restrictions

Laws in many jurisdictions prohibit minors from entering a bar. Cities and towns usually have legal restrictions on where bars may be located and on the types of alcohol they may serve to their customers.

Some Muslim countries, including Brunei, Iran, Libya, Saudi Arabia, and the UAE emirate of Sharjah, prohibit bars for religious reasons. Some other Muslim countries, including Bahrain, Qatar, and the United Arab Emirates, do allow bars but only permit non-Muslims to drink in them.

Types of Bars

A bar's owners and managers will choose the bar's name, décor, drink menu, lighting, and other elements which they think will attract a certain kind of patron. However, they have only limited influence over who patronizes their establishment. Thus, a bar intended for one demographic can become popular with another. For example, a gay bar with a dance floor might, over time, attract an increasingly straight clientele. Or a blues bar may become a biker bar if most its patrons are bikers.

A cocktail lounge is an up scale bar that is typically located within a hotel, restaurant, or airport. A wine bar is an elegant bar that serves only wine (no beer or liquor). Patrons of these bars may taste wines before deciding to buy them. Some wine bars also serve snacks. A dive bar is a very informal bar.

Entertainment

Bars categorized by the kind of entertainment they offer include:

- Topless bars, where topless female employees dance or serve drinks
- Sports bars, where sports fans watch games on large-screen televisions
- Salsa bars, where patrons dance to Latin salsa music
- Dance bars, which have a dance floor where patrons dance to recorded music. But if a dance bar has a large dance floor and hires well-known professional DJs, it is considered to be nightclub or discothèque.

Patrons

Bars categorized by the kind of patrons who frequent them include:

- Biker bars, which are bars frequented by motorcycle enthusiasts and (in some regions) motorcycle club members
- Gay bars, where gay men or women dance and socialize
- Cop bars, where off-duty law enforcement agents gather
- Singles bars where (mostly) unmarried people of both sexes can meet and socialize

Bar (counter)

A row of liquor bottles behind a bar (i.e., counter). The counter at which drinks are served by a bartender is called "the bar". This term is applied, as a synecdoche, to drinking establishments called "bars". The bar typically stores a variety of beers, wines, liquors, and non-alcoholic ingredients, and is organized to facilitate the bartender's work.

The word "bar" in this context was already in use by 1592 at the latest, as the dramatist Robert Greene referred to one in his *A Noteable Discovery of Coosnage*. However, it has been suggested that the method of serving from a counter was invented by Isambard Kingdom Brunel, the great Victorian engineer, as a means of more quickly serving the sudden rush of customers caused by passenger trains arriving at the refreshment rooms at Swindon railway station while the Great Western Railway trains changed locomotives. It has also been claimed that the first bar to serve alcohol was installed at the Great Western Hotel on Paddington station, London. Counters for serving other types of food and drink may also be called bars. Examples include salad bars, sushi bars, and sundae bars.

Locations

Australia

In Australia the major form of licenced commercial alcohol outlet from the colonial period to the present was the pub, a local variant of the English original. Until the 1970s, Australian pubs were traditionally organised into gender-segregated drinking areas—the "public bar" was only open to men, while the 'lounge bar' or 'saloon bar' served both men and women (i.e. mixed drinking).

This distinction was gradually eliminated as anti-discrimination legislation and women's rights activism broke down the concept of a public drinking area accessible to only men. Where two bars still exist in the one establishment, one (that derived from the 'public bar') will be more downmarket while the other (deriving from the 'lounge bar') will be more upmarket. Over time, with the introduction of gaming machines into hotels, many 'lounge bars' have or are being converted into gaming rooms.

Beginning in the mid-1950s, the formerly strict state liquor licencing laws were progressively relaxed and reformed, with the result that pub trading hours were extended. This was in part to eliminate the social problems associated with early closing times—notably the infamous "Six O'Clock Swill" — and the thriving trade in "sly grog" (illicit alcohol sales). More licenced liquor outlets began to appear, including retail "bottle shops" (over-the-counter bottle sales were previously only available at pubs and were strictly controlled).

Particularly in Sydney, a new class of licenced premises, the wine bar, appeared; there alcohol could be served on the proviso that it was provided in tandem with a meal. These venues became very popular in the late 1960s and early 1970s and many offered free entertainment, becoming an important facet of the Sydney music scene in that period.

In the major Australian cities today there is a large and diverse bar scene with a range of ambiences, modes and styles catering for every echelon of cosmopolitan society.

Canada

Canada has absorbed many of the public house traditions common in the UK, such as the drinking of dark ales and stouts. Canada adopted the UK-style tavern (also adopted by the U.S), which was the most popular type of bar throughout the 1960s and 1970s, especially for working class people.

Canadian taverns, which can still be found in remote regions of Northern Canada, have long tables with benches lining the sides. Patrons in these taverns often order beer in large quart bottles and drink inexpensive "bar brand" Canadian rye whisky. In some provinces, taverns used to have separate entrances for men and women.

Canada has adopted many of the newer U.S. bar traditions (such as the "biker bar", and the "sports bar") of the last decades. As a result the term "bar" has often come to be differentiated with the term "pub", in that bars are usually 'themed' and often have a dance floor (such as a dance bar), as opposed to establishments which call themselves pubs, which are often much more similar to a British tavern in style. Before the mid-1980s most "bar" like establishments that sold alcohol were simply referred to as taverns, regardless of what they looked like or what they sold.

As with any major lifestyle trend that occurs in the U.S. the "bar" trend promptly spread to Canada. Canadian sports bars are usually decorated with merchandise and paraphernalia featuring the local hockey team, and patróns watch the games on large-screen televisions.

Starting in the mid-1990s taverns started to take on the look, feel and even the names of the U.K type pubs. A simple example would be the name "The Fox and Fiddle" as a pub name, whereas names like these rarely existed before. There is huge proportion of bars compared to pubs.

Legal restrictions on bars are set by the Canadian provinces and territories, which has led to a great deal of variety. While some provinces have been very restrictive with their bar regulation, setting strict closing times and banning the removal of alcohol from the premises, other provinces have been more liberal. Closing times generally run from 2:00 to 4:00 a.m.

In Nova Scotia, particularly in Halifax, there was, until the 1980s, a very distinct system of gender-based laws were in effect for decades. Taverns, bars, halls, and other classifications differentiated whether it was exclusively for men or women, men with invited women, vice-versa, or mixed. After this fell by the wayside, the issue of water closets led many powder rooms in taverns being either constructed later, or in kitchens or upstairs halls where plumbing allowed, and the same in former sitting rooms for men's facilities.

India

Bars in India are mainly clustered in metro cities, like Delhi, Mumbai, Bangalore, Hyderabad, Goa Manipal etc. Bangalore is sometimes referred to as the city of pubs as there are over 200 bars and pubs located in the city. The state of Goa also has a large number of bars and pubs because of tourism. The rest of the country has very few bar formats.

Mostly, drinks are served in establishments such as restaurants. Locally made liquor (fenny, toddy etc.) is also exclusively sold at establishments. They don't serve traditional liquor but usually serve several snacks and food. These establishments are usually run-down, and their clientele consists mainly of working-class people.

More recently, bars are showing up in smaller cities; but, these establishments cater to a mostly male clientele and are unlike the social hubs of the west. For example, in Chandigarh, one of the most modern city of India, administration has developed Taverns where people can buy liquor at market price and have it along with snacks being served in a decent sitting restaurant that accompanies the wine shop.

In Manipal , many bars serve patrons standing at the counter — no seating arrangements are provided. All the bars are crowded with students

In the last few years, many international brands have entered the market, like 'Hard Rock Cafe', 'TGI Friday's', Ruby Tuesday's', Pop Tate's, 'Ministry of Sound(MOS)', etc. Similar chains of bars are now starting to emerge from within the country. Shalom, Laidbackwaters, Geoffrey's Dhadkkan at Solan, Himachal Pradesh and All Sports Bar are among the few popular ones.

Italy

In Italy, a "bar" is a place more similar to a *café*, where people go during the morning or the afternoon, usually to take a coffee, a cappuccino, a hot chocolate and eat some kind of snack like pastries and sandwiches (*panini* or *tramezzini*). However, any kind of alcoholic beverages are served.

Opening hours vary: some establishments are open very early in the morning and close relatively early in the evening; others, especially if next to a theater or a cinema, may be open until late at night. In larger cities like Milan, Rome, Turin or Genoa, many larger bars are also restaurants and disco clubs. Many Italian bars have introduced a so-called "aperitivo" time in the evening, in which everyone who purchases an alcoholic drink then has free access to a usually abundant buffet of cold dishes like pasta salads, vegetables and various types of appetizers.

Spain

Bars in Spain are very common and form an important part in Spanish culture. In Spain it is common for a town to have many bars and even to have several lined up in the same street. Most bars have a section of the street or plaza outside with tables and chairs with parasols if the weather allows it. Spanish bars are also known for serving a wide range of sandwiches (bocadillos), as well as snacks called tapas or pinchos.

Tapas and pinchos may be offered to customers in two ways, either complementary to order a drink or in some cases there are charged independently, either case this is usually clearly indicated to bar customers by display of wall information, on menus and price lists. The anti-smoking law has entered in effect January 1st 2011 and since that date it is prohibited to smoke in bars and restaurants as well as all other indoor areas, closed commercial and state owned facilities are now smoke free areas.

Spain is the country with the highest ratio of bars/ population with almost 6 bars per thousand inhabitants, that's 3 times UK's ratio and 4 times Germany's, and it alone has double the number of bars than the oldest of the 15-members of the European Union. The meaning of the word 'bar' in Spain, however, does not have the negative connotation inherent in the same word in many other languages.

For Spanish people a bar is essentially a meeting place, and not necessarily a place to engage in the consumption of alcoholic beverages. As a result, children are normally allowed into bars, and it's common to see families in bars during week-ends of the end of the day. In small towns, the 'bar' may constitute the very center of social life, and it's customary that, after social events, such as the Sunday catholic mass, people go to bars, including seniors and children alike.

United Kingdom

In the UK bars are either areas that serve alcoholic drinks within establishments such as hotels, restaurants, universities, or are a particular type of establishment which serves alcoholic drinks such as wine bars, "style bars", private membership only bars.

However the main type of establishment selling alcohol for consumption on the premises is the public house or *pub*. Some bars are similar to nightclubs in that they feature loud music, subdued lighting, or operate a dress code and admissions policy, with inner city bars generally having door staff at the entrance.

'Bar' also designates a separate drinking area within a pub. Until recent years most pubs had two or more bars - very often the Public bar, and the Saloon Bar, where the decor was better and prices were sometimes higher. The designations of the bars varied regionally.

In the last two decades many pub interiors have been opened up into single spaces, which some people regret as it loses the flexibility, intimacy and traditional feel of a multi-roomed public house. One of the last dive bars in London was underneath the Kings Head pub in Gerrard Street, Soho.

United States

In the United States, legal distinctions often exist between restaurants and bars, and even between types of bars. These distinctions vary from state to state, and even among municipalities. *Beer bars* (sometimes called taverns or pubs) are legally restricted to selling only beer, and possibly wine or cider. *Liquor bars* also sell hard liquor.

Bars are sometimes exempt from smoking bans that restaurants are subject to, even if those restaurants have liquor licenses. The distinction between a restaurant that serves liquor and a bar is usually made by the percentage of revenue earned from selling liquor, although increasingly, smoking bans include bars too.

In most places, bars are prohibited from selling alcoholic beverages *to go* and this makes them clearly different from liquor stores. Some brewpubs and wineries can serve alcohol *to go*, but under the rules applied to a liquor store. In some areas, such as New Orleans and parts of Las Vegas and Savannah, Georgia, open containers of alcohol may be prepared *to go*. This kind of restriction is usually dependent on an open container law. In Pennsylvania and Ohio, bars may sell six packs of beer "to-go" in original (sealed) containers by obtaining a take-out license.

New Jersey permits all forms of packaged goods to be sold at bars, and permits packaged beer and wine to be sold at any time on-premises sales of alcoholic beverages are allowed. Historically, the western United States featured saloons. Many saloons survive in the western United States, though their services and features have changed with the times. Newer establishments have been built in the saloon style to duplicate the feeling of the older establishments. Many Irish or British-themed "pubs" exist throughout United States and Canada and in some continental European countries.

Chapter–10

Revolving Restaurant in New Millennium

A revolving restaurant is a tower restaurant eating space designed to rest atop a broad circular revolving platform that operates as a large turntable. The building remains stationary and the diners are carried on the revolving floor. The revolving rate varies between one and three times per hour and enables patrons to enjoy a panoramic view without leaving their seats. Such restaurants are often located on upper stories of hotels, television towers, and skyscrapers.

A barrel-shaped, but stationary, restaurant on Fernsehturm Stuttgart, a TV tower in Stuttgart, Germany, built in 1956, was noted as the inspiration for the idea of a revolving restaurant. A revolving restaurant on Florianturm, a TV tower in Dortmund, Germany, was brought into service in 1959. John Graham, a Seattle architect and early shopping mall pioneer, is said to be the first in the United States to design this sort of restaurant when he created La Ronde on top of an office building at the Ala Moana Shopping Center in Honolulu in 1961. Graham later also used the technology to build the revolving restaurant still in service at the top of Seattle's Space Needle.

BLACK MOUNTAIN TOWER

Black Mountain Tower (previously known as Telstra Tower and Telecom Tower) is a telecommunication tower that is situated above the summit of Black Mountain in Australia's capital city of Canberra. Rising 195.2 metres above the mountain summit, it is not only a landmark in Canberra but also offers panoramic views of the city and its surrounding countryside from an indoor observation deck, two outdoor viewing platforms and the tower's revolving restaurant.

In April 1970, the then Postmaster General (PMG) commissioned the Commonwealth Department of Housing and Construction to carry out a feasibility study in relation to a tower on Black Mountain accommodating both communication services and facilities for visitors. The tower was to replace the microwave relay station on Red Hill and the television broadcast masts already on Black Mountain.

Design of the tower was the responsibility of the Department of Housing and Construction, however a conflict arose with the National Capital Development Commission (NCDC) which, at the time, had complete control over planning within the Australian Capital Territory.

During the approval process of the tower, protests arose on aesthetic and ecological grounds. Some people felt that the tower would dominate other aesthetic Canberra structures due to its location above Black Mountain and within a nature reserve.

A case was brought before the High Court of Australia arguing that the Federal Government did not have the constitutional power to construct the tower (*Johnson v Kent* (1975) 132 CLR 164). The decision was made in favour of the government and construction was able to commence. Telecom Tower was opened on 15 May 1980 by the then Prime Minister, Malcolm Fraser.

Prior to the construction of the tower, CTC-TV (now called Southern Cross Ten Canberra) had its studios located at the top of Black Mountain. Also located on the top were two guy-wired masts, one for CTC7 and the other one for the local ABC TV station. These were demolished in 1980 after the tower had opened

Facilities

Black Mountain Tower provides vital communication facilities for Canberra along with both indoor and outdoor observation decks, a café and a gift shop as well as the revolving Alto Tower Restaurant. There are three floors of business, sales and radio communication facilities located between the 30.5 metre and 42.7 metre levels providing space for communication dishes, platforms and equipment for mobile services within the tower.

The viewing platforms provide 360 degree views of Canberra and the surrounding city and countryside. Visitors to Black Mountain Tower can see the city unfold from the enclosed viewing gallery or from the two open viewing platforms. Besides the telecommunications facilities the tower includes also a souvenir shop, a relaxing coffee lounge, and Canberra's only revolving restaurant which rotates 360 degrees in 81 minutes which allows diners to experience a different view throughout their meal.

In the lower level of the Tower's entrance foyer, there was formerly an exhibition "Making Connections" which traced the history of Australian telecommunications from the earliest days into the 21st century but this has since been removed. There is a theatre which provides a video, produced shortly after the tower opened, on the tower's design and construction.

Black Mountain Tower has become one of the most symbolic landmarks in Canberra and a major tourist attraction with a total of over six million visitors. In 1989 the World Federation of Great Towers invited the tower to join such distinguished monuments as the CN Tower in Toronto, Blackpool Tower in England and the Empire State Building in New York. Black Mountain Tower is one of the most visually imposing structures on the Canberra skyline, visible from many parts of Canberra and Queanbeyan.

SURFERS PARADISE, QUEENSLAND

Surfers Paradise is a suburb on the Gold Coast in Queensland, Australia. At the 2006 Census, Surfers Paradise had a population of 18,501.Colloquially known as 'Surfers', the suburb has many high-rise apartment buildings and a wide surf beach.

The feature of the central business district is Cavill Mall, which runs through the shopping precinct. Cavill Avenue, named after Jim Cavill, an early hotel owner, is one of the busiest shopping strips in Queensland, and the centre of activity for night life. Surfers Paradise's high-rise buildings are the best known feature of the Gold Coast's skyline; Burleigh and Coolangatta also have skyscrapers, though shorter and fewer.

WESTIN BONAVENTURE HOTEL

The Westin Bonaventure Hotel and Suites is a 112 m (367 ft), 35 storey hotel in Los Angeles, California, constructed between 1974 and 1976. Designed by architect John C. Portman, Jr., it is the largest hotel in the city. The top floor has a revolving restaurant and bar.

It was originally owned by investors that included a subsidiary of Japanese conglomerate Mitsubishi Corporation and John Portman & Associates. The building is owned by Malaysian businessman Francis-Edward Bonaventure, managed by Interstate Hotels & Resorts (IHR), and is valued at US$200 million.

Chapter–11

Food Service and Gourmet Coffee

Food service (US English) or catering industry (British English) defines those businesses, institutions, and companies responsible for any meal prepared outside the home. This industry includes restaurants, school and hospital cafeterias, catering operations, and many other formats.

The companies that supply food service operators are called food service distributors. Food service distributors sell goods like small wares (kitchen utensils) and foods. Some companies manufacture products in both consumer and food service versions.

The consumer version usually comes in individual-sized packages with elaborate label design for retail sale. The food service version is packaged in a much larger industrial size and often lacks the colorful label designs of the consumer version.

Food service sales to restaurants and institutions are estimated to be approximately $400 billion, about equal with consumer sales of foods through grocery outlets. Major food service providers include Aramark, Brinker International, Compass Group, the Crown Group, Darden Restaurants, Sysco, McLane Company, US Food service and 3663 First for Food service.

EMPLOYMENT STATISTICS

The food service industry is one of the largest employers in the United States. Over 805,360 people are currently working as servers and managers alone. 59% of these workers are under the age of 30, and over 66% hold only a high school diploma or less.

Counter Service

Counter service is a form of service in restaurants, pubs, and bars where food or drinks are ordered at the counter. Counter service is also called "bar service" in the case of pubs and bars where the counter is also called the bar. Counter service is compared with table service where service is provided at the table.

With counter service, the customer generally pays before consuming the food or drink. Some fast food restaurants offer only counter service while table service is the common form in most restaurants. For pubs and bars, bar service is the norm in the United Kingdom and the Republic of Ireland whereas table service is the norm in the United States and Continental Europe.

Table Service

Table service is food service served to the customer's table by waiters and waitressess, also known as "servers". Table service is the norm in most restaurants, while for some fast food restaurants counter service is the common form. For pubs and bars, table service is the norm in the United States whereas counter service is the norm in the United Kingdom. With table service, the customer generally pays at the end of meal. Various methods of table service can be provided. See, for instance, silver service.

Gueridon Service

Gueridon service is a form of food service provided by restaurants to their guests. This type of service encompasses preparing food (primarily salads, main dishes such as beef stroganoff, or desserts) in direct view of the guests, using a "Gueridon". A gueridon typically consists of a trolley that is well equipped to prepare, cook and serve the food to the guest. There will be a gas hob, chopping board, cutlery drawer, cold store (depending on the trolley type) and general working area.

FOOD SERVICE'S THEORY OF EVOLUTION

Harland Sanders was nearing desperate straits when in 1952 he visited Leon W. "Pete" Harman in an effort to persuade the Salt Lake City restaurateur to sell his specially seasoned chicken.

After 13 years of perfecting an herb-and-spice chicken recipe at his roadside restaurant, Sanders, a former streetcar conductor and justice of the peace, recently had learned that he was going to be a former operator as well. The new interstate 75 was planned to bypass his hometown of Corbin, Ky., taking with it much of the traffic that had patronized the long-popular Sanders Court & Cafe.

So Sanders, then 66 years old, hit the road, lugging his secret recipe, a pressure cooker and a lofty plan to make his fortune by allowing other restaurateurs to add his chicken to their menus in return for a few cents each time the product was sold. Harman, who knew a good deal when he tasted it, obliged. Together, the two pooled their talents and began to build the world's largest quick-service chicken chain.

"I was the first franchisee, so it was a handshake thing," recalls Harman, founder of 264-unit Harman Management Corp. in Los Altos, Calif. "There were no other documents floating around."

In the 46 years since then the relationship between KFC Corp. and its franchisees has grown far more complex. As the chain took flight and the white-suited colonel became one of the country's most recognizable icons, several suitors came looking for their share of the proceeds. Along the way the rules of empire-building changed. and the simple franchise relationship vanished forever.

Investors Jack Massey and John Y. Brown bought the business during the 1960s, and Heublein stepped up to the plate in 1971. Each purchase tested the franchisor-franchisee bond, but it was after PepsiCo Inc. made its bid in 1986 — six years after the beloved colonel's death — that the relationship nearly hit the skids.

In 1989 Harman — the man who coined the phrase "Kentucky Fried Chicken" and soon after had the evolutionary idea to put the chicken in a bucket with potatoes, biscuits and gravy and market it as a meal — joined other franchisees in a bitter legal battle over a new franchise contract. The dispute raged on for seven years, crippling the trust that had helped the system thrive. The company, which now operates 9,000 outlets worldwide, still is working to recapture the fragile balance of franchisor and franchisee interests crucial to longevity.

"One thing we all recognized is that we couldn't settle without it being a win-win for both parties," David Novak, former head of KFC and current leader of KFC-parent Tricon Global Restaurants, said when the settlement was announced. "But our job really has just begun. There's more pressure on us now to work closer together."

KFC's growing pains are by no means unique or isolated. As franchise systems have matured and competition within the food service industry has increased, many a chain has found itself plagued by the dual challenges of continuing to grow a concept without choking the livelihoods of existing franchisees.

The widespread use of nontraditional locations only complicates the conundrum.

"The challenge today has less to do with franchising than it has to do with different segments of the industry," says Larry Hantman, senior vice president and general counsel for Randolph, Mass.-based Allied Domecq Retailing USA, which operates the Dunkin' Donuts, Baskin Robbins and Togo's chains.

"As the industry matures, the number of franchised units in any one segment increase and competition intensifies," Hantman explains. "So individual franchising systems have to keep concepts alive, keep them meeting consumer expectations and keep them vibrant.

"Franchising works best when it's growing," he continues. "It's a business, and the major challenge is not to get involved in the internecine battle on how you divide the pie, but how do you grow the pie? Is the product all it can be? The constant striving for excellence within the system — that is the challenge."

SEWING UP A NEW KIND OF DEAL

Widely accepted as the fastest means by which to distribute a product, franchising has proved over the decades to be both savior and sore spot. While many people have struck it rich linking their destiny to a franchise system, many also have kissed their life savings goodbye. Just as surely, franchisors imbued with honest dreams of creating thriving and mutually beneficial enterprises have been undermined by crooks perpetuating scams that depleted the wallets and souls of unsuspecting victims.

Today franchising accounts for nearly 41 percent of all retail sales in the United States, or $800 billion annually, according to statistics published in 1996 by the Washington, D.C.-based International Franchise Association. The group estimates that there are about 550,000 franchised businesses in the United States alone, employing 8 million people. And, the IFA estimates, a new franchise opens every eight minutes.

STEPS FOR SUPERB GOURMET COFFEE

For a change, a fantastic cup of coffee would definitely be great. It does need some time and plenty of energy to locate a great cup of fine coffee these days. Should you know the perfect cafe, you are one of the fortunate ones. Although, did you know that you can certainly basically make a great cup of gourmet coffee within your own from home?

Here are seven straightforward tips which you may do to build the excellent cup of coffee every time. Set up with excellent quality. One of the most critical facets of coffee consumption is the rating of the coffee that an individual start with. In case an individual have a choice flavoring, then acquire whole beans in that taste. If you can certainly do this, it will make it possible for a person to acquire probably the most fresh coffee available.

Mill away. Get a reputable coffee mill. A number of of the ideal mills for sale today are easy to work with and simple to clean up. By means of grinding your personal coffee beans, you may be given the option to only mill what you require, signifying that you may have complete quality in your gourmet coffee.

Keep It Proper And Firm. It is very critical to place

your coffee securely. Air oxidizes the coffee and can allow it to get sour easily. Steel bins can also permit a metal taste to get directly into the coffee, making it taste bad.

The main answer is for a plastic-type or ceramic air tight carrier for your coffee and coffee beans. In addition, store it at room temperature simply because the wetness in the refrigerator or freezer can make it go bad quicker.

BIBLIOGRAPHY

• Aguilera, Jose Miguel and David W. Stanley. Microstructural Principles of Food Processing and Engineering. Springer, 1999. ISBN 0-8342-1256-0.

• Campbell, Bernard Grant. Human Evolution: An Introduction to Man's Adaptations. Aldine Transaction: 1998. ISBN 0-202-02042-8.

• Carpenter, Ruth Ann; Finley, Carrie E. Healthy Eating Every Day. Human Kinetics, 2005. ISBN 0-7360-5186-4.

• Davidson, Alan. The Oxford Companion to Food. 2nd ed. UK: Oxford University Press, 2006.

• Food and Agriculture Organization of the United Nations. The State of Food Insecurity in the World 2005.

• Howe, P. and S. Devereux. Famine Intensity and Magnitude Scales: A Proposal for an Instrumental Definition of Famine. 2004.

• Humphery, Kim. Shelf Life: Supermarkets and the Changing Cultures of Consumption. Cambridge University Press, 1998. ISBN 0-521-62630-7.

• Jango-Cohen, Judith. The History Of Food. Twenty-First Century Books, 2005. ISBN 0-8225-2484-8.

• Lawrie, Stephen; R A Lawrie. Lawrie's Meat Science. Woodhead Publishing: 1998. ISBN 1-85573-395-1.

• Magdoff, Fred; Foster, John Bellamy; and Buttel, Frederick H. Hungry for Profit: The Agribusiness Threat to

Farmers, Food, and the Environment. September 2000. ISBN 1-58367-016-5.

- Mason, John. Sustainable Agriculture. Landlinks Press: 2003. ISBN 0-643-06876-7.

- Mead, Margaret. The Changing Significance of Food. In Carole Counihan and Penny Van Esterik (Ed.), Food and Culture: A Reader. UK: Routledge, 1997. ISBN 0-415-91710-7.

- Merson, Michael H.; Black, Robert E.; Mills, Anne J. International Public Health: Disease, Programs, Systems, and Policies. Jones and Bartlett Publishers, 2005.

- Messer, Ellen; Derose, Laurie Fields and Sara Millman. Who's Hungry? and How Do We Know?: Food Shortage, Poverty, and Deprivation. United Nations University Press, 1998. ISBN 92-808-0985-7.

- Nicklas, Barbara J. Endurance Exercise and Adipose Tissue. CRC Press, 2002. ISBN 0-8493-0460-1.

- Parekh, Sarad R. The Gmo Handbook: Genetically Modified Animals, Microbes, and Plants in Biotechnology. Humana Press,2004. ISBN 1-58829-307-6.

- Regmi, Anita (editor).Changing Structure of Global Food Consumption and Trade. Market and Trade Economics Division, Economic Research Service, USDA, May 30, 2001. stock #ERSWRS01-1.

- Schor, Juliet; Taylor, Betsy (editors). Sustainable Planet: Roadmaps for the Twenty-First Century. Beacon Press, 2003. ISBN 0-8070-0455-3.

- Simoons, Frederick J. Eat Not This Flesh: Food Avoidances from Prehistory to the Present. ISBN 0-299-14250-7.

- Smith, Andrew (Editor). "Food Marketing," in Oxford Encyclopedia of American Food and Drink, , New York: Oxford University Press, 2007.

- Van den Bossche, Peter. The Law and Policy of the bosanac Trade Organization: Text, Cases and Materials. UK: Cambridge University Press, 2005. ISBN 0-521-82290-4.

INDEX